THE DEBT DIET

FINANCIAL FITNESS STRATEGIES FOR EVERY INCOME LEVEL

SHANNA BARITOT

SHANNA BARITOT

ISBN: 979-8-9922804-0-1 (Paperback)

ISBN: 979-8-9922804-1-8 (Hardcover)

Book Cover by Robert Harrison

Seneca Author Services

First edition: 2025

DEDICATION

This book is dedicated to my sister, Malika. I will never stop being proud of you, and this book is for both of us.
I hope you know that despite it all (or maybe because of it all), we turned out ok. And your nephews?
Ohh, how beautifully they're growing up to become such good men.
You'd be just as proud of them as I am.

'And all these diamonds that you left for me
That I just thought were sand'
-Sean Rowe

FOREWORD

Remember when we were growing up... and in English class, we had to learn how to write in cursive? Impressive! And in Social Studies, we learned all about the birth and development of our country? Fascinating. In Earth Science, it was all about the rocks. And in Math class, the importance of long division and trigonometry? Good times. And in Personal Finance, how to effectively manage your money? Invaluable. And in Chemistry, the smell of...wait...can we go back to the money one? Ummmm...I don't recall that one now that I think about it.

Wait a second...how can it be possible that for most of us, learning how to be a good steward of our money is left to trial and error? Or from the colleague at work who just leased (aka rented) that stunning new car for only $525 a month? Or the friend who needs their starter house to have those granite countertops they've always dreamed of?

Meanwhile, we are constantly being bombarded with easy credit and messaging that we somehow *deserve* to enjoy that thing we can't pay for right now. That's ok...just finance it. You know...debt is just normal. Worry about how to pay it back later.

While there are certainly examples of truly unfortunate circumstances that can lead to a heavy debt load, the truth is that most of it is directly related to our *behavior*. And unfortunately, our behavior can lead us down a path into a debt pit. The credit card usage leads to balances that can't be paid off in full. Which leads to ridiculous interest charges. Which prevents you paying down the principal even though you're making payments. When you finally wake up to the reality that the lenders aren't looking out for *your* best interest, the light bulb will probably go off. And when those lights go on and you make the decision to change your path, then your life will change. Don't believe me? Well keep reading...it's worth your time.

Signed,

R.C.C.

October 2024

DISCLAIMER

This book is not intended to be a substitute for financial advice from a professional in this field. All information presented in this book comes from my own personal experience and what worked for me. You should always consult a financial advisor for specific questions about your own situation, as needed.

CONTENTS

CHAPTER ONE

STEPPING ON THE SCALE

B efore the day that I made the decision to get out of debt, I honestly believed I had my finances under control. Looking back on that now, I have no idea how I ever convinced myself of this – it was so far from the truth. There was even a time (thankfully many years ago) when my only 'budgeting' strategy was to simply avoid checking my mail for a few days. And no, I'm not kidding. I'd even managed to justify this since it was usually bills I didn't want to deal with, or catalogs I couldn't afford so I just...spread it out a little. That is, until I accidentally got one of my neighbor's catalogs – I still can't fully look her in the eye without an inner chuckle (seriously though, atta *girl!*).

As long as we're admitting things we probably shouldn't admit, I also used to put everything but my bills on a credit card without ever paying more than the minimum payment each month. It was also 'normal' to stretch out my car loans to the longest term allowed, just to make my payment smaller. The price of the car didn't even matter back then – just the lowest monthly payment. I cringe now when I think about how much I must have paid in interest on those loans (and others with a similar strategy). I wouldn't even keep the car for the full loan term, and was once so upside down that I had to roll all that remaining debt into a new loan. But back then, it was how I got by.

Please understand that I am not proud of any of this – I remember every ounce of what it felt like when I had to put some of my groceries back because the total started to exceed my bank balance and my credit card was at its limit. That shame burns from a place that runs deep, adding a layer of stress that many of us don't even realize we're carrying. But the kicker is, *nobody talks about any of this.* Talking about money is taboo, and stress over money ruins more relationships than people care to admit. So we suffer in silence and just learn to live with it, like I did for a very long time.

The crazy part about all of this is that despite all of these ridiculous strategies, I still somehow never felt like my financial life was a mess. It all just seemed...normal to me. There wasn't a lot of financial success in my family and I had no formal financial education to speak of. Growing up, we struggled to make ends meet – those two 'ends' never quite touched in our house. Selling jewelry and living out of a cooler when the refrigerator broke for a month? That's not 'making ends meet.' In hindsight, we were in survival mode, and doing the best we could.

But it wasn't until I started getting out of debt that I finally began to understand how much my upbringing shaped the way I handled money as an adult. Going from paycheck to paycheck was just how we did things back then, and I had never questioned any of it. I distinctly remember thinking how great it would be to reach a point where you didn't have to look at a price tag because the price didn't really matter. That was so unfathomable to me back then.

I mention all of this here because *you* may not consciously realize how much of your own upbringing you carry forward into your adult life if you're not careful. Both the good and the bad. I had unintentionally and blindly carried so much of this into my own adulthood, so relatively speaking, I really thought I was doing just fine. I was one of the very few in my family that went to college and the first (and still only) to have received a master's degree. *Magna cum laude*, I might add – though it took me years to allow myself to really be proud of this. I did not come from a place that placed much importance on education. However, not really knowing better and certainly having no alternatives, I financed that degree with just shy of $100,000 in student loans that I had been carrying for fourteen years by the time I started getting out of debt. *Fourteen years*, and I had barely made a dent in the principal by then.

In the rooms of recovery for those with experience in this area, people talk about hitting their 'bottom' – what finally made them ready to change their lives for the better. I believe that financially, this can either be a single event, or possibly 'debt by a thousand cuts.' It's all those times you've felt frustrated with your bank overdraft fees, or felt ashamed for not being able to afford whatever that thing is you can't pay for because your cards are maxed out. Or not being able to go to the ATM for the simple reason that there is nothing *in* there to take *out*. Maybe it's knowing you're being paid less than your education and experience lends itself to simply because you need health insurance...all of it. Sound familiar? Sometimes just wondering how the hell you can make so much money, but still have so little to show for it is enough to get started. Whatever prompted you to pick up this book, I promise it goes up from here.

Some of you may have never hit any of those 'bottoms' I talked about above. Or, mine may pale in comparison to yours. Most likely though, you may not feel like there is a problem at all but part of you *knows* you make far too much money to have so little in savings (and so many payments). Maybe you've never considered that you're still carrying your student loans from your Ph.D. despite having such a successful career.

You may even be like I was thinking, why not? I don't really 'need' to do this, but it probably can't hurt.

This book is for anyone – no matter your income level – who wants to improve their finances. As a society, we rarely talk about money – it's one of the three taboo topics we're taught from a very young age never to bring up in polite company: money, religion, and politics. Because of this, many of us have never had any education or even positive examples about handling money. Our parents were likely doing the best *they* could with the tool set they themselves were given – I know mine were. And since nature abhors a vacuum, that gaping knowledge void will inevitably be filled with some potentially terrible advice. Everything I brought into my adult life when it came to handling money came from a very unexamined place of survival mode, but it wasn't until the day I decided to get out of debt that I truly understood this.

That day, specifically, was September 14, 2017. That was Day One. My then-husband and I had driven down to NYC to see a concert (the ridiculously talented Brandi Carlile if you're wondering), and we listened to an audio book on the way down that happened to be about money. There are so many books like this out there, so the name of that particular book is irrelevant, though we will forever be grateful for the springboard it turned out to be. We had each read other books about finance over the years prior to (and after) this, but this one just happened to be the one we were both ready to 'hear' that day.

We both agreed that even though we 'weren't really in debt,' it couldn't hurt to look at our finances when we got home and see if there was any room to get a little more financially fit. We even agreed that we probably wouldn't have to make too many changes because we really were 'doing great' but why not try it, right? This turned out to be a gross understatement of *massive* proportions. Comically massive, obnoxious, full-on-denial proportions that we still laugh about now.

We had what would become our first ever budget meeting over drinks one night shortly after we got home. Or more accurately, I believe we started that budget meeting and then quickly decided cocktails might help because this can be a really touchy conversation (putting it lightly). We listed every debt we could think of, verbally and then on paper when the list got unexpectedly (and alarmingly) lengthy. We even joked that since I only had one credit card that I paid off each month (thankfully now several career upgrades removed from when this was my only means of paying for things), and he had one with just a small balance, we didn't really 'need' to do this but why not, right? Ohh my goodness how very wrong we were. When we finally wrote out all the things we owed money on, it was sobering – and more than a little nauseating. We clearly weren't in the *least* bit financially fit and did, in fact, genuinely need to do something about this.

I think of that moment as finally **stepping on the scale** for the first time – you truly have no idea of your own financial picture until you do this and can see in bold and unforgiving numbers exactly what your debt weighs. It's the first thing you do when you're trying to lose weight for a reason – how else are you going to know how much weight you have to lose? The analogy holds very true here – **weigh your debt.** All of it. I'll say that again: *all* of it. Stand there buck naked or in your cute little skivvies if you must, but weigh out *every single thing* that you owe money or have a payment on. This process is deeply uncomfortable but it's only once you finally do this – and let me tell you, it was like a battering ram to the gut when we realized just how *much* we owed – that you can finally begin to come up with a plan to lose that financial weight. The goal of this book is to show you exactly how we did that, and to save you some of the pain of my (tremendous) learning curve. I'll also share some of the many lessons and insights I learned, and I'll provide you with immediately actionable tips you can start doing right now, *today*, to get out of debt for good.

Throughout this book, I'm going to be candid, vulnerable, and very transparent about the process that led to an entirely different and much healthier relationship with money, for both myself and my children. Where it makes sense, I'll talk about concrete numbers, but for most part I won't because my income may differ significantly from yours – and that's completely beside the point. Anyone can do this at any income level; this process has everything to do with what you *do* with your money rather than how much you *make*.

I'll methodically walk you through the steps we took to eliminate all of our debt (I'll get to the specifics of exactly how much that was later) in the hope that you can apply these strategies to your own life. It will require sacrifice and introspection, but I can promise you that it will be *so worth* the journey. Because let me tell you, the **5 years, 3 months, and 5 days** it took to get from that concert drive to the moment we hit 'send' on the last payment on our mortgage December 19, 2022 were worth every single bit of will, determination, tears, arguments, shame, and ultimately triumph to experience what being debt-free feels like. And I would wish this feeling on everyone. I promise you, if you decide to start and simply don't stop, you will get there too and it most definitely *will* be worth it.

Before we begin though, it's worth addressing who I am (and who I am not), and what business I have speaking about any of this. I am not a financial professional, though I completed a fantastic financial coaching program some years ago. What ultimately helped me get out of debt was a mix of various books, authors, articles, airport conversations, people I admired, financial professionals, etc., and then even further customized to what actually worked for *me* – some of which differs from all of that. I hold degrees in Business and Education but ultimately, even those are irrelevant to this book you're now holding. What *is* relevant is this: I am someone who worked really damn hard to get out from under a *mountain* of debt, for a very long time, and I learned a tremendous amount about myself and this process. That, my friends, is the only qualification that matters here – I did this, and so can you. And brace yourself, because I'm going to share every ugly and wonderful detail of that process with you (with advance apologies for any swearing, and there will be swears). So let's fucking *do* this.

Chapter Two

Weighing the Debt

I don't know who needs to hear this, but just because you can make the payments for something doesn't mean you can actually afford it. Should I say that again for the people in the back? Maybe stand on a chair and shout it? Trust me on this. It really doesn't. Before we get into what constitutes debt, it's worth a mention that *none* of what I'm laying out here comes with judgment. Please trust me when I say that I fully understand the shame that comes with debt, particularly debt you may have carried for a long time. Perhaps from a degree you never finished, or debts from a period of personal struggle (job loss, divorce, debt from a funeral home for unexpectedly having to pay for your loved one's burial with no savings for such a thing). I get it. If you can't tell, I am speaking very candidly and from painful personal experience with all of this and as such couldn't be less judgmental about any of it. My one genuine and heartfelt request here is that you give yourself grace. What matters is not *how* you got here, but where you *go* from this point forward. It absolutely can and will get better – it just starts with deciding to begin.

So, here's where we strip down to our fiscal birthday suit and get ready to step on the scale. What constitutes debt, then? It's easy to think of the obvious student loan payment, or the credit card balance. But there are so many other areas that we don't even think about as debt. In my own experience, when we first looked at our finances, I had to realize that even our car leases, a home equity line of credit (HELOC) for a kitchen remodel, and my son's braces payment plan were all part of the picture. Hear me out – for so many of us, **debt has been completely normalized.** To the point that we can look at the neighbor with the big, shiny new truck pulling the even bigger and shinier new camper and think – *yes.* They've made it. We may even *know* that they have a monster payment on those 'toys' (likely because people are weirdly proud of such things and tell us this) but even still – they are *doing* this!

Wait – let's break that down for a second. Have you ever stopped to wonder at what point we convinced ourselves that the bigger and shinier the toys that someone has, even when we *know* they carry such a large payment, the better someone's financial situation must be? Isn't that completely backwards logic? Or that the fancy and expensive car in someone's driveway means they are winning at life? All that really means it that they likely have a huge financial obligation to a lender who could repossess the vehicle if they miss even one payment. Until the loan is fully paid off, the lending institution owns that vehicle, not them. I say all of this to demonstrate that *anything at all* with a payment on it constitutes debt. In simplest terms, **payments = debt.**

So this is how you're going to determine what to put on that scale. While that seems like an obvious and unnecessary thing to say, there are so many hidden debts sprinkled throughout the month – or even once per quarter or year payments – that you just don't think of. Note here as well – there really are no 'bad' or 'good' debts – this is simply math. Do you owe money on it? Then it's debt. Over the first year, we kept uncovering debts of all different kinds that were either subscription payments we forgot about or were for things you don't traditionally think about as a stereotypical debt. Some examples of 'hidden' debt from my own experience:

- Cell phone payments on your bill: that new cell phone isn't 'free' – add up what you still owe and count it as debt

- Dental work payments (or medical payments for programs such as CareCredit which thankfully exist for very good reason)

- Home Equity Line of Credit (HELOC) loans: remember, your house is collateral for these

- Personal loans of any kind (in our case, from a camper and camping property we rarely used anymore)

- 401(k) loans: while this is worth a section all its own by those with expertise in this area, all I will say is to be so careful here – borrowing from your retirement can cost you, both in taxes and your future financial security

- Car payments

- Student loan payments

- Basically, *anything* with a payment on it – no matter how low

Speaking of car payments, let's talk about leases for a moment. I was always taught – always – that a lease is the 'least expensive' way to own a car. You get 'more' car (read: newer) for 'less' money (read: lower monthly payment). Technically, both are true. However, you never stop paying for your car – you're only paying someone else for the depreciation of that vehicle plus applicable rent and taxes, with nothing to show for it at the end of the lease period. There certainly are some pros here: you can upgrade your vehicle every 2-4 years. You only pay the sales tax on your actual depreciation, not the full price of the car. You can ease the financial burden of repairs since much of this is covered under warranty, and you're likely getting a safer vehicle simply based on how new the car is with up-to-date safety features. Your down payment to secure this lease is often lower than buying a car or may not even be required. Note, however, that often no down payment simply means the financing institution is rolling that upfront payment into the bulk of your lease.

However, the cons for leasing are much lengthier and with larger negative financial implications. The mileage requirements seem minimal when you agree to 'only' pay 10-50 cents per mile over your allotted annual mileage (usually 10,000-15,000/year), but for a lot of people this turns out to be a significant financial burden when they've exceeded this mileage by thousands of miles. Sometimes a job change or a move during the lease period can add up to significantly more driving than in previous years, even when you estimated based on past usage. You may also be responsible for excessive wear and tear that you would otherwise overlook if you owned the car yourself. Insurance premiums are potentially higher since you're insuring a higher-value vehicle. And what many don't realize – we certainly didn't – is that often there is a 'loyalty' penalty of $500 or more that is incurred if you don't upgrade your lease with the same vehicle manufacturer.

If you have a car or lease payment, add it to your debt list. From here, you have a choice to make. You can pay it off quickly, trade it in for a less expensive vehicle, or, as I did, downgrade your car entirely and buy a used one with cash. In fact, I think this is such an important point that I devote a section of Chapter 9 to explaining *how* you can get rid of car payments permanently and only pay cash for your vehicles going forward.

It's worth repeating here that none of these 'payments' are inherently bad or good. Listen, subscription services to the YES network for us

11

Yankees fans might be considered an absolutely necessity in one house but complete blasphemy (if you cheer for the wrong team, of course) in another. I kid! No really, don't stop reading here if you're a Red Sox fan – calm down. Go sports. But it's important not to label debts as 'good' or 'bad' because that only leads to negative self-talk. That's just not helpful, and an excellent way (and excuse) to stay stuck.

The goal here is to help you make positive, forward movement towards financial freedom. We've all heard that saying that the best time to plant a tree was 20 years ago but the *next* best time to plant one is today, right? That's exactly what we're doing here – and it can only go up from here. Haha see what I did there? Up? Like a tree? Yes! Ok, I'll stop. I should probably warn you here though, that if you can't tell already, I constantly amuse myself and I'm very easily amused. I'd apologize, but I'm not actually sorry for that because I am *hilarious*.

Joking aside, here is where you'll tally up the total balances of what all of those payments are attached to and put them on the scale. *This*, my friends, is the weight of your debt. Sit with this number for a minute here – it's probably not a fun realization. We were absolutely floored by the weight of it, honestly. Remember when I mentioned that we didn't really 'need' to get out of debt but that this process 'couldn't hurt'? It turned out that what we owed was more than *two years' worth of my entire salary* (before taxes). And that didn't even include our mortgage, to give you a sense of how much we had to pay off. That was a deeply uncomfortable realization. I had taken out just shy of $100,000 in student loans for my master's degree in 2004 that I had barely made a dent in. That was nearly fourteen fucking *years* prior at that point, and I had so far paid almost $35,000 in interest and counting. No matter what *your* total debt is, I hope you'll allow this realization to prompt some tremendous (and very positive) changes.

So when you find yourself wondering how you can make so much yet have so little to show for it, *this* is where your income is leaking. It is scattering in the wind with all the payments, interest, and finance charges we pay on all this debt we carry around. Take this amount and write it down (there are even apps to help keep track of your debt amount). This list is the foundation for everything else we'll do.

Note that in listing your debt at this stage, this shouldn't yet include your mortgage if you own a home *unless* you aren't current on those payments. That absolutely should be made current first if necessary, and I will fully defer to a financial professional in your life for the best advice here since that's well outside the scope of this book (but very, very important to address). Assuming you are current on your mortgage and choose to get rid of this as well to become fully debt-free (as we did), this will go in line but only after all the other debt is gone for good. You'll continue making your regular monthly mortgage payments in the meantime.

The goal of this book is to show how we got rid of every financial 'pound' on that scale. Every. Single. One. You'll find that I'm staying with the 'diet' and 'scale' mentality because the parallel is hard to ignore here (and because it amuses me). We've all heard of crazy diets – popsicle diets, water diets, baby food diets, cotton ball diets (yes, really) – but ultimately even these get a toe hold, albeit briefly, because some of them work initially. Why is that? Because that person is measuring their intake and outgo of calories (er, cotton balls) for what may be the first time, ever. See the parallel here? In this case, you're measuring your financial picture on paper for what also may be the first time, and by doing so, you have officially begun this process. (Also, please don't start eating cotton balls – that is absolutely not what you should be getting from that example.)

In the next chapter, I'll show you how to make a budget and ultimately 'stop the bleeding' with all these payments. I promise you, there is a weight that comes with debt you may not have realized you've been carrying until you finally set it down, and the freedom that comes with shedding that weight is exhilarating.

CHAPTER THREE

THE BUDGET, THE SPRINKLER, AND THE FIREHOSE

FIRST, THE BUDGET

Quick – what's your income? I'm guessing most of you had a number come to mind pretty quickly. We all know what we make so I would hope that was an easy question. So with that in mind...as quickly as you can think of it, what's your 'outgo'? In other words, how much do you spend per month, including bills and everything else? Do you need a minute? Or an hour with a calculator perhaps? Hell, do you have *any* idea at all? That's not a judgment – I had no idea of this number when we started all of this and wasn't even in the *ballpark* when I guessed what we spent on dining out or even groceries every month. Most people don't – even to within a couple hundred dollars or more. Which is crazy, given that it's so important to our financial health. But that's exactly why so many of us have simply accepted this feeling of knowing we make too much to either be this broke, or have so little in savings. Or maybe we have plenty of discretionary income, but we still have so many monthly payments. Sound familiar?

Remember when we were kids and we learned to 'stop, drop, and roll' in elementary school? For good reason, this was drilled into our heads throughout our formative years. But most of us were never taught how to balance a checkbook, how to buy a home, how to avoid credit card debt, etc., and while we've never been on fire, most of us have been in debt for *years*. Well, I mean some of us have been on fire for various reasons (that's a pretty great story for another day), but you get the idea. We're taught so many things growing up that many of us will never have to apply in the real world, but we are never taught solid money management; we are *woefully* unprepared for this part of adulthood (and it shows). This is partly what led to this book – I know this would have helped with my own learning curve when getting out of debt had something like this existed, particularly the mindset shift. I'll even take that one step further and say that if I had a solid financial education of sorts growing up, perhaps I wouldn't ever have gotten so deep into debt to begin with.

Here is where budgeting comes in. Let's be very clear here – budgeting does not mean you have to start extreme couponing or cutting out all the 'fun' things in life like world travel or going out for fancy dinners. Or...maybe it will – it's entirely up to you, your goals, and your timeline. I can promise you I am not going to judge if your household budget includes a very hefty Amazon Prime line item (mine does). Listen, you can budget for filet mignon or you can budget for ramen noodles and Twinkies, my friend. Your goals, priorities, and the speed at which you choose to get out of debt will determine this. Our budget was flexible over the five years it took us to get out of debt. We kept it at a comfortable level for a while, indulging in things that were important to us as needed. Given my sons' ages at the time, we made a choice to include a bigger travel budget because we all love to travel (and I will continue to ride this period where they still want to travel with me until the wheels come off). But there were also times that we tightened it up significantly when we got tired of making slower progress, or when we had a specific goal in mind. Flexibility and a deep understanding of where *you* stand are key.

Now, after stepping on the scale in Chapter 2, it's time to look at where your money is going. Simply put:

1. Start with your income
2. List every single one of your expenses
3. Subtract your income from your expenses

For your income, be sure to include anything regular coming in – all jobs, side hustles, front hustles, Social Security, etc. – whatever you can count on monthly. For expenses, include both regular and irregular expenses (quarterly HOAs, annual insurance payments, etc.). Don't forget things like gas and entertainment – all the ways you're spending your money qualify for this category. I found that the best way to do this was to export my bank statement to a spreadsheet. There are even great apps that can help you categorize your expenses and how much is being allocated to each, or you can do this a little more old school with a pen and paper.

When first starting out, it helps to look at perhaps a 3-month period to average this out. Group similar expenses (groceries, dining out, etc.), or create columns in Excel and use a pivot table to categorize your spending. You don't have to go that far – just group similar items on paper and total them. This total represents your expenses for any given month. At first, we're not making any changes here – we are just measuring for your initial budget.

Once you have your expenses, list your income in one column and your expenses in a second column. Again, include all income sources – any money coming in – and total that too. Determine what these totals are for a month at a time. Now, subtract your expenses from your income.

This amount that you have left over at the end of the month becomes what you're going to use to knock down your debt. Give me a minute and we'll get to that. But it's all at once this complicated, and this simple.

When you first do this, that 'leftover' amount may be in the negative and that's ok for the moment – this is the whole reason you're doing this (and may be a big part of the reason for much of this debt). We're calling this your *initial* budget because at the end of all of this, your budget is going to look much, much different. Ultimately, you're going to get rid of all of those debt payments on that list of expenses and free up so much more of your income.

We're initially just trying to determine where all of your money is going because that allows you to see where cuts can be made (and please trust me, the first time you do this especially, they absolutely *can* be made). It was eye-opening to see how much we were spending on groceries and then even more on dining out – you know, because we had 'no food in the house.' Or worse, I stuck it in that black hole that normal people refer to as their freezer (I really do need to get better about this). Once you have created a budget showing your income and expenses clearly, you'll be ready to start tackling your debt.

THEN, THE SPRINKLER

A big part of what I learned throughout this process (and what really kept me in debt) was that I was doing it all wrong when it came to paying off debt pretty much my whole life – though with the best of intentions. I think most of us are. I came to think of what I used to do as the **sprinkler method**: I'd pay a little bit here and there whenever I happened to have 'extra' in my bank account. But just as only a little bit of the lawn gets a little bit wet with a sprinkler – and only when the sprinkler is aimed directly at it – only a little bit of our debt is getting a little bit knocked down when we do it this way. And all that time, interest and finance charges are happily growing like weeds while the sprinkler is pointed in another direction. Do you see how this really only *kinda* works?

What actually works – and please understand, this allowed me to pay off that $100,000 in student loans I had been carrying for fourteen years – is what I came to think of as the **firehose method**. It's called a lot of things in a lot of different books, but this is what makes the most sense to me. A firehose is much, much more powerful and focused than a sprinkler, right? (I used to be a volunteer firefighter and that analogy always amused me so just humor me here.) The firehose method lets you aim all that extra money between your income and your expenses directly at the base of your debt, starting with the smallest one, until it's gone. It's incredibly satisfying to watch this happen. If you take nothing else away from this book, at least *try* what I'm about to lay out for you and see how much momentum you'll gain in a fairly short amount of time. I promise you'll never go back to using the sprinkler method again.

AND NOW, THE FIREHOSE

To get started paying off your debt with the firehose method, here's what you're going to do:

- In the 1st column, list out all of your **debts** based on the total amount that you owe, smallest to largest

- In the 2nd column, list the **total amount owed**

- In the 3rd column, list only the **minimum** monthly payment due (I'll explain this in a minute)

- In the 4th column, list your **firehose payment** (firehose payment = income – expenses), which is what you'll use to pay off the debt

- In the 5th column, track your running **total debt owed**

Note: You can get cute and add those other columns too like I did to show the math (and momentum), though this isn't needed unless it makes your little nerd heart happy, too.

It will look something like this:

Debt Listing	Total Amount Due	Minimum Payment	Firehose Payment	Minimum Payment + Firehose Payment	Breakdown	Total Debt Owed
1. Credit Card #1	$ 250	$ 200	$ 50	$250 → $0	Min pmt #1 + extra $50	$ 89,185
2. Student loan #1	$ 5,322	$ 300	$ 250	$550 → $0	Min pmt #2 + extra $250	$ 88,935
3. Car loan	$ 7,210	$ 350	$ 550	$900 → $0	Min pmt #3 + extra $550	$ 83,613
4. Credit Card #2	$ 8,303	$ 410	$ 900	$1,310 → $0	Min pmt #4 + extra $900	$ 76,403
5. Credit Card #3	$ 10,100	$ 500	$ 1,310	$1,810 → $0	Min pmt #5 + extra $1,310	$ 68,100
6. Student loan #2	$ 58,000	$ 800	$ 1,810	$2,610 → $0	Min pmt #6 + extra $2,610 until DEBT FREE!	$ 58,000
						$0!!!

For the purposes of this illustration, let's say you have $50 extra left over at the end of the month once you've done your budget and subtracted your expenses from your income. You'll start with paying **minimum payments only** on all of your debts. Take that **firehose payment of $50** and add it to the minimum payment for your smallest debt ($200 in this example), making it **$250**. Continue to do that until it's paid off. Feels great, right? *This* is where the magic happens.

Now look at row 2 – your **firehose payment just grew to $250 because debt #1 is gone**, so add that to the minimum payment for your next debt. If that minimum payment is $300, you'll now pay **$550 toward debt #2** ($300 + $250) until it's gone. *Nothing else has changed* – our income is the same, our expenses are the same, but we now have much more 'extra' power behind that firehose. Once #2 is gone, the **firehose payment becomes $550**. Isn't that crazy? Keep going!

Once you've paid off debts #1 and #2, add that $550 to the minimum payment for debt #3, making it **$900/month** ($350 + $550). Once debts #1, #2, and #3 are gone, #4's payment becomes **$1,310/month** ($410 + $900). With no other changes to your budget, your **firehose payment is now $1,310!** And so on, with each debt you eliminate freeing up more money for the next until you're debt-free.

This, my friends, is how you get out of debt. You gain so much momentum when you're only aiming the firehose at one debt at a time and paying the minimum payments *only* on all the other ones. Can you see why this is so, so much more powerful than the sprinkler method of scattering a little bit extra here and there but not really making much progress anywhere? This is focused, powerful, and absolutely will knock out your debt one perpetually growing payment at a time until you are debt-free. As long as you keep going and refuse to stop, you will get out of debt doing it this way. And I promise, it'll be amazing.

Note that I listed only your minimum payment here – we are not factoring in interest at all. I know, I know, *Shanna, that's crazy because this one credit card I have has a really high interest rate, this doesn't apply to me, I'm special, blah blah*...I know, I know. I *get* it. I was there too, remember? But this process is about momentum and very simple math on purpose. That mentality of trying to game the system was part of what kept *me* stuck for years. I'd 'sprinkle' a little more money here and there using exactly that logic and ultimately made no progress anywhere. When we switched to this process and stayed with it, we finally became debt-free. So, I am telling you from personal experience that this works and at the very least, it's well worth a try.

You can always go back to your way and you will absolutely not offend me. Hell, I won't even know. But isn't the definition of insanity doing the same thing over and over (and over), but expecting a different result? Once you pay off that first debt, the momentum is incredible. And when that debt is gone, you'll have more room in your budget to keep going. There may be exceptions, of course, depending on your specific circumstances. Debts that may be in collections, time-sensitive payments, and in particular, mortgage payments if they are past due come to mind. Because these are all outside the scope of this book, I'd strongly encourage you to speak to a financial professional for advice about any extenuating circumstances you may have.

As you do this, celebrate each and every 'win' you have along the way – this was my ex's idea and I absolutely loved it. There are so many – paying off a debt, cutting an expense, or anything that moves you closer to your goal. We used to keep a bottle of champagne with a sticky note on it labeled 'the next win' and open (then replace) as we saw fit. I still do actually, because sometimes you just need to celebrate that life is *good*. Whatever you do, make sure you acknowledge your progress to stay motivated. And you get to decide what constitutes a 'win' for you – how great is that? If you're doing this by yourself, see if you can find an accountability partner that will both support and celebrate with you along the way – and call you on your bullshit.

In the next chapter, I'll talk about all the different ways I've used (and continue to tweak) for cutting my expenses down to find more room in the budget for that firehose you'll be throwing at your debt. But first, take a moment here to congratulate yourself for getting this far. For many of us (myself very much included), this may well be the first time ever in our adult lives that we've actually made a budget and really worked at taking care of ourselves financially. And because you cannot manage what you do not measure, you've taken the first step toward changing your financial future. Kudos, my friend. Truly.

CHAPTER FOUR

THE TIPS!

I f you're anything like I am, when I read a book like this, I will shamelessly go to the table of contents and skip right to the 'good stuff.' I see all of you, skipping Chapters 1-3! I'm not even mad – I do it all the time. But even I have to say that this time, don't skip straight to this section. Or if you do skip to this chapter because you also hate being told what to do (same, same), then read it because it's full of useful information, but then I truly encourage you to go back and understand the beginning. Ultimately, there's a *reason* we all got into debt in the first place and that reason is as varied as our backgrounds and personalities. Understanding why we got into debt is crucial, and acknowledging this helps shift towards a healthier financial mindset. This shift is key to not only getting out of debt, but staying out for good.

That said, welcome to the chapter that prompted me to write this book. My goal here is to provide you with very specific, immediately actionable tips and tricks that ultimately helped me get rid of every single penny that I owed. I've discovered simple ways to 'find' extra money in my budget every month and I want to help you avoid some of the mistakes we made back then. My learning curve was steep – there were things I didn't really understand until months or even *years* into this journey – and I'd like to help save you the pain of some of those mistakes.

So – I'd encourage you to start by simply looking around. Your house, your kitchen, your driveway, your closet...all that 'stuff' – every single piece of tangible property that you own – used to be money, my friends. Ouch, right? Quite simply, here is where your answer ultimately lies when you wonder how the hell you can make so much yet have so little to show for it. Have you ever purchased anything that didn't *quite* fit your hot, sexy body but didn't want to be bothered with returning it? Or worse – things you bought and never even wore/used/ate or hell, *found* again? That may never have even had the tags taken off and are hanging in your closet as we speak? Money, wasted. The lesson here is that your possessions may be a reflection of poor spending habits. Whatever emotional void you may have been trying to fill with that one when you drunk-shopped...it didn't. No? Just me? Haha, fair enough.

Getting rid of things you no longer need can free up space and change your shopping habits. It helped me reorganize my home and reduce the urge to buy more. It even helped me to better organize my house when I stopped having to store so much stuff. Did you ever notice that you don't actually appreciate anything more when you have to buy a storage bin to put it in and then shove it under your bed? Have you ever cleaned out a closet or a room and you just felt somehow...lighter the next time you walk in? That's the feeling that I'm talking about. I even read somewhere once that things hold energy – some very positive and some less so when attached to a more painful memory. Perhaps that's one explanation for that feeling of lightness. Or perhaps that's all bullshit, I don't know. But whether you believe that or not, it's a good exercise to go through.

Now, on to the tips! (I feel like there's a joke in there somewhere that I am going to choose to ignore.) There are many paths to getting out of debt. Mine may look similar to yours or entirely different depending on the amount of debt you have, your income, values, motivation, and goals. Given that the end goal is the same though, what follows are a few of the areas where we found some pretty significant savings in our budget.

You ultimately have two choices: you can either increase your income, or you can widen the gap between your income and expenses by cutting down your expenses. For the latter in particular, there are tons of little ways to do this. Cumulatively, they all really add up – particularly when you realize that even saving $10 per day on nonsense adds up to $3,650 per year. You're essentially taking a crowbar (a Halligan, if you will) and steadily widening that gap between the money you have coming in, and the money you have going out. There are so many ways to do this:

- *Coffee*: If we are in-real-life friends, you know that I shamelessly love coffee. To the point that I have an industrial-style Keurig that's plumbed into the water line in my kitchen. I'm not even sorry – coffee is amazing. But my ex and I realized we were going through quite a bit of coffee when we both worked from home for a time and that we were spending $920/year in K-cups back then. That's not even including what I spent hitting up my favorite coffee shop – that was just the coffee we were drinking at home. That's...a disturbingly large amount of money that we'd never really paid attention to before. Once we realized how much we were spending on this, we started using refillable pods and good quality beans to grind and saved quite a bit of money this way. Or shop for coffee in bulk or use the ol' drip coffee maker. And before you get all judgmental on me, some of it *is* decaf, for the record (though probably not nearly enough, to be fair).

  o The key lesson is this: if there's something in your life (coffee, shoes, Amazon Prime, whatever) that you tend to indulge in...measure it. Put it on the scale and weigh it. Then consciously decide if this is worth all the money you spend on it *or* find a way to cut this down (or out). We found coffee wasn't worth almost a thousand dollars a year, so we made changes.

- ○ *Coffee, part two* (because I obviously have a problem): Get whatever the ingredients are for your most favorite, most perfect, happiness-in-a-cup drive-thru latte creation – syrups, creams, caramel drizzle, even reusable 'to go' cups, whatever makes your heart happy – and make them at home. This equals immediate savings multiplied by however many times you (didn't mean to) go buy a coffee. You can even buy an inexpensive and cute little frother to make it fancy. Stop judging me, it's very unbecoming of you (actually, go ahead – I really do drink too much coffee).

- *Cable*: Cable can be expensive. Consider cutting it or shopping around for better prices, especially if you're renting equipment from the company. Sometimes calling them for a better price works, but it's often worth checking alternatives. But hear me out – if the NFL network is worth its weight in gold to you, keep it. Just consciously *choose* to keep it versus simply paying a lot for channels you may not use and may not have realized how much you were paying for (again – put it on the scale and weigh it, then decide).

- ○ *Cable, part two and more to the point*: Pick just *one* streaming service, love the hell out of it, silence your phone to watch it whenever you want, and cancel all the rest.

- *Price matching*: Shop around – the bigger the item, the bigger the potential savings here. I found my dog's monthly flea treatment elsewhere for significantly less than the company I usually order it from. I asked my current company if they'd price match instead of simply switching companies and they *did*. Who knew? You really do miss 100% of the chances you never take and it's always worth an ask.

- *Selling things around the house*: All that stuff used to be money, right? Turn it back into money, then. I sold a vintage ring on eBay for $700 that I hadn't worn in years. It's crazy what you have sitting around that may well be worth more to someone else than it is to you (particularly if it's just in a closet or under a bed). We sold a beautiful set of Amish wooden furniture we were simply storing for several hundred dollars, an old Tiffany lamp, a few fancy purses I never used, and even equipment or tools we had in the garage that we weren't using. Use your imagination – there's a lot you can do here if you're motivated, and many different platforms to sell through. It all adds up.

  o *Selling things around the house, part two*: Have a garage sale. Make everything – every single thing – negotiable to get rid of it. Anything you make is more than what you had five minutes ago and can be thrown at your debt. Or donate it and take a tax write-off. Or do a little bit of both.

- *Side hustles*: Explore ways to make extra money. Donate plasma, take part in clinical studies, or use platforms like Upwork, Uber, Lyft, and Door Dash (check on your auto insurance risk here though with your company or agent). If you're motivated, there is so much out there. Deliver pizza, wait tables, walk a dog, babysit. Dig deep, there are so many ways to make money that are limited only by your imagination and motivation level.

- *Or... 'front hustles':* What is a front hustle, you may ask? This ridiculous (and slightly amusing) term is your main income, folks. This is where you're going to get the most bang for your buck – find a way to use your **primary** source of income in overtime, consulting, or freelance work, if possible. I know nurses who travel or do private home care for clients. I know electricians who make a quite a bit in side jobs. I also know quite a few in law enforcement who do or have done private security. That's going to be your biggest leverage and source of additional income. Hell, negotiate a pay raise if you can. When's the last time you did that? This process may also prompt you to realize you really need to up your income overall and perhaps look at a new job/field/career. Only you can decide that but the point is, see what you can do to maximize your income since that's going to be your biggest leverage in getting out of debt.

- *Cooking from the freezer and pantry:* You can save *so* much money by simply using what you already have before buying more. Such a simple concept, but I'm terrible at this. Most frozen food has a shelf life anyways, and I don't know about you but the moment I freeze something without cooking it right away...it is no longer in my life. It is dead to me. I swear to you – I might as well have thrown it away, never to be seen again. I *hate* thawing food – I don't know why – and yes, I know I have issues. Plus, it's out of sight, out of mind. Try taking inventory of your food to avoid unnecessary purchases.

- *Meal planning:* It is amazing how far this goes, and I know some people who are simply amazing at this. In full disclosure, you should know that I am *not* one of them. You'll need to go find one of their books because you won't find any great wisdom here about that. But even I know know that it's well worth even some simple planning to maximize both what you have on hand (see above), and what you buy. Bonus points if you meal plan for the next day or two with leftovers, too. Double and triple bonus points if you bring it to *my* house so that I don't have to cook (I'll bake for you as a thank you – that one is my love language!).

- *Buying meat in bulk*: Take ground beef for example. I freeze it in 1-2 lb. portions in a gallon freezer-safe zip bag, flattened out so that it thaws more quickly once I'm ready to use it. I think this is the only thing I actually *do* use my freezer for like a (fairly) normal person. Or even better, support your local farmers and buy directly from them. If you're a meat-eater, split a larger quantity of local farm-raised meat with friends if needed – you'll get huge quantities this way although, see my freezer dilemma above as a word of caution.

- *Grocery shopping at different stores*: In addition to couponing – here again, not my expertise but some people have made this an art form – simply watching ads and shopping at different stores for different items can save you quite a bit of money. Use apps to check online prices while in-store. Big box stores are great for bulk items, while farm markets can offer cheaper, fresh produce. Look into farm shares too.

- *No spend weeks*: I see you, Amazon. It's amazing how automatically we shop (online in particular) without thinking about it, out of boredom or even to fulfill a need that has little to do with actually needing that item we're buying. Make this slightly more difficult by putting something in your cart and waiting a couple days to see if you still really want or 'need' it when the initial impulse has passed. Usually you don't. Or if you do, sometimes that store will offer you a discount for said item because they recognize that it's in your cart.

- *Apps*: Speaking of shopping, *remove* apps on your phone that make it easy to spend money. Obviously I love Amazon Prime (if you can't tell), but if there is an app you use often to shop, perhaps remove the app and only shop from their website on your computer. Just add a little more friction to make it more difficult to do it automatically.

- *Paying in cash only*: It's very easy to spend money when you don't 'feel' it. This is different for everyone – personally, I hate spending cash. I rarely carry it so when I do, I don't like to spend it. Yet I have no problem at all using my debit card. For my younger son, it's the opposite – he prefers to spend cash because he knows his bank account balance is going down with every swipe of his debit card. Whatever your personal pain point is, use *that* to spend money. Using cash can help you feel the impact of your spending. It also forces you to stick to a budget and limits impulsive purchases.

- *Warranties*: It is so tempting to always tack on the 'only x amount' warranty – whether it's for trip protection, the newest iPhone, or for a car. I've learned to go deep on the fine print because often what you want to be covered – let's say, wear and tear on an expensive leather sectional – *won't* be covered in that add-on warranty they're selling you. Obviously, I'm speaking from personal experience, there too. So a lot of times, I'll make a conscious decision to 'self-insure' instead of buying the warranty, particularly considering that most purchases have some period of manufacturer warranty already built in for any defects or failures. Meaning, I'm making the decision to just pay out of pocket for any repairs that may eventually be needed beyond that built-in warranty period. That said, some items are very worth the warranty given the price point of what you're buying. An after-market warranty we purchased on our older cars saved us thousands of dollars for repairs, for instance. Insurance on bigger ticket items such as trips with travel protection – particularly international – might also be highly recommended; research the best options here, go deep on reviews, and shop around. Ultimately, do the math and your research to determine if it might be worth it to pay out of pocket if needed versus throwing more money at a warranty you're not entirely sure will cover what you need to cover anyways.

- *Higher deductibles*: Another potential savings area involves raising your deductibles on your insurance plans – the one caveat being, you need to be able to set something aside to pay the higher deductible if ever needed. Additionally, paying your insurance premiums 6 or 12 months at a time once you're able to versus monthly can save you quite a bit on your policies.

- *Insurance*: Speaking of insurance, have your policies reviewed each year to ensure that your coverage is both adequate for your insurance needs and that you're getting the best rates. I'll talk about this and the deductibles more in the next chapter.

- *Books*: Self-proclaimed book nerd here – I love them. But I've saved money by using apps like Libby to borrow books and audiobooks for free. Local library cards give you access to a vast selection of books and audiobooks through these apps without subscription fees. You can also get a library card for the biggest city in your state (most allow this, search online) and connect to that library too for a much larger selection. Or – go to the actual library, same idea.

- *Avoid being house- or rent-poor:* I did this exactly once in my life, and never again. Quite simply, don't buy a house or rent an apartment at the top end of what you can afford, or even that you're pre-qualified for – so, so much in savings here. If you're always stretched thin with a mortgage or rent payment, how are you ever going to find room to save?

- *Staycations:* I love to travel. Truly *love* to travel. I have a sinking fund just for this (more on that in Chapter 9). But while getting out of debt in particular, there is something amazing about saving tons of money on airfare/hotel/rental cars and for a fraction of that cost, acting like a tourist in your own city. Spend a week locally doing movies, dinners, cocktails, bowling, axe-throwing, hiking, whatever – something different every day. Google 'best things to do in (insert your city here)' and you'll be amazed at what you don't even know is in your backyard. Even with indulging here and there, you'll still spend far less than on most vacations.

- *Storage units:* Hear me out here. Sometimes they're needed but a lot of the time, they really aren't. I did this once and it's not something I'll ever do again so this is where I'm coming from – obviously I realize there will be a lot of exceptions to this. I once paid to store a couch and a bunch of other things that after a year or so, were musty, dusty, and no longer things I even wanted when I moved into my new place. In the simplest of terms (exaggerating on purpose here), if you pay $100/month, that's $1,200/year to store a couch that may not even *fit* in your new place – either physically or with your décor – so perhaps take that $1,200 and save it to buy something that will when the time comes. Even if it's red and leather if that's who you are by then, you just never know.

- *Subscriptions*: Look at all of them. Which ones are actually improving your life in some way? Can you cut any? Maybe just one? Or five? No? Are you *sure*? Come on, challenge yourself!

- *Monthly expenses*: List out all your monthly expenses and look at anything recurring. Even small amounts add up so challenge yourself to cut out anything unnecessary. I think you'll find there is quite a bit of fat that can be trimmed here.

In the end, these are temporary sacrifices for a much bigger, long-term goal. You can do this. In the next couple of chapters, I'll dive into even more significant savings areas.

CHAPTER FIVE

INDEPENDENT AGENTS

T his one deserves its own chapter because the savings can be tremendous here. Having worked in the insurance industry for many years, I thought I was pretty savvy when it came to getting the best rates for my car insurance. I'd shopped around online and used the price comparison tools, and I was happy enough with what I had. Granted, the rates continued to go up each year but still – it was good enough.

Then, I came across an interesting concept regarding captive versus independent insurance agents, which I hadn't fully grasped before. Prior to shopping online on my own, I had worked with an insurance agent who represented a single company. Meaning, he was a captive agent that was only able to offer rates for that specific insurance company. This explained why my rates would continue to climb each year – he could only shop around for me within the confines of his own company.

When we began working toward our financial goals, including eliminating debt, we decided to see if we could save on insurance. We were referred to an independent agent, who, unlike a captive agent, could shop across the marketplace for us without being bound by any one company. He's now been my agent for several years. His office took a complimentary look at the car policies we had at the time and provided us with an auto insurance quote that provided not only better rates than we'd had but even more importantly, better and more comprehensive coverage.

Because of this, we had him look at all of our policies. At the time, this included two auto policies, a homeowner's policy, a motorcycle policy, a camper policy, and two life insurance policies. Because he wasn't bound by any one specific company but the marketplace as a whole, he ended up saving us money on *every single policy* without exception – to the tune of $1,260/year in savings. And it wasn't just about lower rates – it was about better and more comprehensive coverage, too. For those who don't feel like doing the math here, this meant we had added an extra $105 to our firehose every month to fuel our financial progress.

Very worth noting is that all of this came at no cost to us. Independent agents earn their commissions by selling and servicing policies, so their services are free to the customer. Which happens to be another benefit – they'll walk you through any life changes or potential claims if ever needed. They will also review your policies annually – again at no cost to you – to be sure you're still getting the best coverage and rates. There is simply no downside to this.

As we continued tightening our budget, we also started experimenting with our insurance deductibles. The deductible, if you're unfamiliar, is what you pay out of pocket on a claim if ever filed before your insurance company pays the rest. This can range from a very small amount to over a thousand dollars depending on the type of policy and your coverage limit (which is the maximum your insurance will pay in the event of a claim). The lower your deductible, the higher your monthly premiums because the insurer assumes more of the financial burden. If you're willing to take on more of that risk, a higher deductible means lower premiums. A policy with a $100 deductible is going to have a much higher premium than one with a $2,500 deductible, for instance. The trick here is making sure you have enough savings to cover the higher deductible should the need arise.

Finally, many insurers offer discounts if you choose to pay for a longer-term premium upfront. If you're willing and able to pay for six months or a year in advance, you can often avoid the administrative fees that come with paying monthly. While paying monthly is perfectly fine, especially when you're focusing on paying down debt, this is another area where you can save money down the line when the time is right.

In summary, insurance doesn't have to be a 'set it and forget it' expense. By working with an independent agent, adjusting your deductibles, and paying premiums annually, you can see significant both savings and better coverage, getting you that much closer to debt freedom.

CHAPTER SIX

CELL PHONE SAVINGS

A nother huge savings area that we found in our own budget was with our cell phone bill, so this one also deserves a chapter all its own. If you're like most people, your cell phone bill is probably one of the largest monthly expenses, right after housing and food. On the plus side, this means that it also represents one of the largest potential savings areas in your budget.

When we first started paying attention to our budget, our Verizon bill was a whopping $220 a month for a 4-phone plan. Worth repeating – that's $220 every 30 *days*, or $2,640 per year. Though we weren't exactly happy with that amount, we paid that for a long time. We'd even occasionally commiserate with other people about it, but we never really did anything about it because...well, what other options did we have, right? This way of thinking created what I think of as 'blind spots' or 'leaks' in our budget – those areas where money slowly slips out of your account and you don't even realize it until you really take a hard look at your finances. Once we started looking more closely at all the places our money was going, we realized there was a lot of room for improvement.

So, we decided to find ways to tackle our cell phone bill. It was not always a smooth process, and I'll try to spare you some of the pain we went through. My (then) teenage sons did not love the data that suffered throughout this process. And please note, these are all great companies we're about to discuss. I am not promoting or hating on any of them – just sharing my own very transparent experience with each, which can even be different geographically depending on the companies' saturation of cell towers in other areas.

1. Our first change was to T-Mobile. At the time, T-Mobile was still growing its network in our area, and while our bill dropped significantly from $220 to $150 per month, the coverage definitely suffered. My son and I would be sitting on the couch side by side and I had no service while he had full bars. Or one of the teenagers' Wi-Fi would cut out during a 'really important' moment in a video game (I know, the horror). We were willing to put up with a lower strength signal periodically, but it wasn't long before we realized this wasn't sustainable. I'd give this one a 'D' overall for my service area, though I hear they've made huge improvements since then. So, if you're considering them now, don't rule them out completely.

2. Next, we decided to give AT&T a try. The one downside was having to replace our phones with AT&T-compatible phones (which is why most people probably never make this switch). To make the switch, we bought unlocked phones with carrier-specific SIM cards and that worked out well (Verizon didn't require this but AT&T and others do, or at least did back then). You can even look for a refurbished phone with a warranty, which will probably get you the best price overall. Once we did this, every carrier we tried since that initial switch has been compatible

with AT&T's cell towers, so it was a one-time hurdle (albeit kind of a pain in the ass). AT&T was a definite improvement over T-Mobile. Our monthly bill was a little higher at $160/month (though still much better than $220 we had been paying), but we had virtually no coverage issues other than the occasional concrete or underground venue, and AT&T's much wider reach of cell towers rivaled Verizon's signal strength.

3. Then we happened to hear a radio ad for Pure Talk Wireless. Turns out, Pure Talk uses the same cell towers as AT&T and the monthly rates were even better at $120/month. While we were all admittedly a little gun-shy after our T-Mobile experience (and said teenager was absolutely not thrilled about trying a new carrier again), we made the switch without issue. New SIM card, same phones, and it was a seamless transition. We were all happy with this one so we stayed here for awhile.

4. But as we continued fine-tuning our budget, we decided to make one more tweak after hearing about Visible. Visible uses Verizon's cell towers but represents massive savings over Verizon. At this point, I will admit that even I didn't want to change carriers again. I figured what we had was good enough, great even, given the monthly savings we'd found with strong cell coverage. But I can honestly say that the transition was almost seamless to Visible. The monthly cell phone bill came down to exactly $100/month for 4 phones inclusive of all taxes and fees(!). And on a very funny note when out shopping, a salesman tried to pitch me on another carrier's plan. I just smiled and told him I was very happy with Visible, and this man – without missing a beat – *shouted* after me that if I ever decided to pay more,

he'd be happy to help! It made me laugh out loud – how could you not love that kind of sense of humor? He clearly knew all about Visible, but two ladies shopping nearby stopped me to ask me what this Visible was all about. This one is a well-kept secret worth sharing. So if you have this in your area, it is very worth a look.

It's worth repeating in case you were multi-tasking and didn't catch that: we saved *$120 per month* (that's $1,440 per year, folks!) when we finally decided to look at our cell phone bill, and it was worth every bit of the trial and error we had to go through. Plus, there are no contracts with Visible, so you can leave whenever you want – no strings attached.

In addition to the monthly savings, it's a powerful feeling when you realize you have so many choices in life. Even though it may feel like it sometimes, you are never truly stuck – financially or otherwise. I've since made what seems like millions of little tweaks to my finances through these types of changes even to this day, and they've all been worth it.

✢

CHAPTER SEVEN

DINING OUT

S pending money on dining out also deserves its own little chapter (bite-sized, if you will – get it?). For us, this was a *huge* money leak. Until we stepped on that scale and measured what we were spending here, we really had no idea how much money was being spent (wasted) on restaurants every month. Not. Even. Close. And listen – if this is really something you enjoy, it's perfectly ok to make this part of your budget. If you're hitting that coffee shop every few days, maybe do that only on weekends at first. Or – get the exact ingredients they use to make your favorite fancy beverage and make it at home. (Are you getting a sense of where one of my personal pain points was? Remember that time I mentioned how much I love coffee?)

But here again, be *intentional* about it and measure just how much money you're spending in this area to be sure it's in line with your financial goals. In addition to how much we were spending on groceries, we were spending quite a bit on restaurants for really no reason other than not wanting to cook any of those groceries we just bought (or I had put them in that black hole of a freezer), or as a default social outing with friends.

Once we started focusing on our finances, we realized we could scale this back without sacrificing the social side of dining out. For example, cutting out alcohol or appetizers at restaurants saves a significant amount on the bill. Or, we could switch our social events to having friends over for a potluck instead of dining out – same idea but significantly less expensive. I still love to entertain, and I'm sure you do too, so this was a great way to stay social while being more budget-conscious.

The list of ways you can find to save money is as endless as your imagination, and the more motivated you are to get out of debt quickly, the more this list will grow. Challenge your partner to do the same, and your kids, or talk to your friends to see what they do. In fact, I did just that for you in Chapter 14 and talked to a lot of people who were willing to share a hell of a lot of great tips! That turned out to be one of my favorite chapters of this book because I love hearing how different people handle their own finances. You'll find that it becomes very motivating once you start seeing the needle on your debt start moving into slimmer territory, and you'll find some crazy ways to speed up this process. In the next chapter, I'll talk about the *biggest* savings areas we found in addition to all of these smaller ones already discussed – one of which knocked out an enormous chunk of debt in one fell swoop.

CHAPTER EIGHT

THE CAMPER, THE HARLEY, AND THE CARS

B y far, the biggest place where we found savings was sitting in our driveway, so this one gets its own short chapter too because the savings were tremendous here. This not only took a crowbar to that space between our income and expenses when we removed all of these payments, but it also took out a *big* chunk of debt all at once.

Remember when we talked about looking around and realizing that all of your 'stuff' used to be money? You probably have some pretty big-ticket items that may have seemed important at the time but could actually be a huge roadblock to your financial freedom. For us, the realization that we could sell some of these items to get rid of debt hit us hard. I'm talking about things like our camper and Harley Davidson – items that once seemed like symbols of success but ultimately just added financial strain.

Here again, this mindset shift is going to be directly in proportion to how quickly you want to get out of debt and ultimately, it's about long-term gains over short-term inconveniences. You absolutely can be the guy with the gorgeous 5th wheel camper in your driveway, but you may eventually decide that you'd rather be the guy that's debt-free *and* has a gorgeous 5th wheel camper in your driveway. I'm not even going to pretend that's an easy decision, but...we did exactly that. Not at first, of course. This was one of those realizations that took a little time to sink in and for us to get comfortable with for the greater purpose of getting out of debt.

We made the tough decision to sell our camper and deeded campsite when we realized how much it would shorten our timeline to becoming debt-free. Selling this knocked out a significant chunk of our debt at once (*21% of my annual income* at that point, to be specific). Thinking about it in terms of the percentage of my salary made the impact crystal clear. The camper was honestly painful to let go of – we spent a good amount of time there when the boys were younger in particular but we weren't spending as much time there as we used to. And given our financial goals, it just felt indulgent to keep. We also knew we could make the decision to buy another camper once we were out of debt, and this time, without a payment attached to it.

A few months after that, we realized we could do the same thing by selling our Harley. I'm not even going to pretend that I was as deeply affected by this decision as my ex – but here again, our goals were bigger than the idea of having a Harley in the driveway. Damn, she was pretty, though! But in the end, letting go of these big-ticket items gave us the financial freedom we needed to keep moving forward and significantly increased the money we were using to pay off our debt.

These decisions weren't easy to make, but they were some of the most powerful ones that we made on our journey to being debt-free. And who knows? Once you're debt-free, you can always buy that camper or Harley again – this time, without the payments. Selling that Harley in particular also helped us cash flow our first paid-for car and we never looked back. In the next chapter, I'll explain exactly how we got rid of our car payments, permanently.

CHAPTER NINE

EMERGENCY FUNDS, SINKING FUNDS, AND ELIMINATING THE CAR PAYMENTS

We've covered quite a bit at this point, and I realize I've given you a lot of 'homework' as well as a lot of information to take in. Hopefully, if you're still with me, you've started your budget – and this will change and evolve quite a bit throughout this process. You've gone through and listed out any and all debts that you owe. You've sorted them in order from smallest to largest and you're making only the minimum payments on everything in order to begin. Hell, you might even have begun the process of knocking them out with your first 'firehose' payments so far. Hopefully you've also started combing through that budget to look for any fat you can trim out of your expenses to add to that firehose. Now that you're here, we need to talk about emergency funds.

EMERGENCY FUNDS

An emergency fund, ideally, is going to help you stop borrowing money so that you can focus on getting rid of what you already owe. We all know that life happens, and having a cushion to rely on if necessary is going to help quite a bit. At this point, you're going to want to set aside $1,000 earmarked solely for emergencies, not to be touched unless absolutely necessary. I think of this as my 'in case of emergency, break glass' money – and most things don't qualify to break that glass. A survey done by *CNBC* found that 63% of workers are unable to pay for a $500 emergency – it's no wonder so many of us are in credit card debt.

The ideal amount for this *initial* emergency fund will be $1,000 because many minor financial emergencies will fit inside of that. Having this money set aside will allow you to cash flow whatever it is you need without having to put it on a credit card. If you ever do have to tap into this fund, you'll then halt your debt payoff *very temporarily* while you replenish your emergency fund back up to $1,000.

Your circumstances may call for a modification to this if your income and expenses are much lower or higher, but the bare minimum should be $500. Even with a significant income, however, you'll still want to aim for this $1,000 because all we're trying to do here is stop borrowing until you're debt-free. This has to kept separate from all other funds as a true emergency fund though, and not touched for anything outside of those types of circumstances. Doing this breaks that continual and vicious cycle of getting any further into debt.

SINKING FUNDS

With that taken care of – and seriously, congratulations for getting this far – let's talk about sinking funds and handling money proactively instead of reactively. For me at least, the latter was really the only way I ever did things. Credit card bills would come for things I had completely forgotten I'd charged nearly a full billing cycle ago, and I was always unprepared to pay them in full. Utility bills would always stress me out even though yes, logically, I realize these are monthly bills and they show up every 30 days. And each year, come birthdays or holidays, the monthly checking account would take a hit for these 'unexpected' expenses even though they were never 'unexpected.'

But I would spend money simply because it was in the account without ever setting anything aside for things like this, as foolish as that sounds. Ridiculous, isn't it, the things we do to ourselves? I was just never planning ahead, financially. It's so easy to get into this trap of feeling like you're a victim of your own stupid choices (speaking for myself here) if you don't have a bigger goal to aim for. Once that goal became debt freedom for me, it changed everything. This is where **sinking funds** come in.

One of the first sinking funds we created was out of necessity when we started paying the homeowner's insurance premium yearly for the discount. Since that's not a small amount of money, we divided that annual premium by 12 months and started making a monthly 'payment' to ourselves into a new savings account opened just for this. This account was even (very cleverly) labeled 'insurance sinking fund' to keep this separate from other bills. We later upped this to include the annual premium for the auto insurance policies as well, so these didn't come as a surprise either.

You kind of have to back into these amounts based on when they're due and build it accordingly. $1,200 due in 12 months will look like a $100/month payment to this account, but $1,200 due in four months will look like $300/month so that when they're due, it's there. Down the road, if you find an account that pays you interest for what's in these accounts, great. But for now, keep it simple and find a way to set this money aside so when these bills come, the money will be ready to go.

We also created a gift fund for Christmas gifts, birthdays, etc., based on how much we anticipated spending in this area and opened another savings account earmarked just for this. If you own a house and don't escrow your taxes, this 6-month or 12-month bill is also expected and should have a sinking fund to help prepare for that eventuality as well. I'm still surprised by how much peace it gives me never having to stress about bills like this – they once used to sideline me because I was simply never prepared.

Your own personal circumstances and priorities are going to dictate your sinking funds. One of the priorities that matters quite a bit to me is traveling with my sons before they're all the way grown and flown. And this precious time that they actually want to spend time with me? Hell yes, I will ride that until the wheels come off. Since we all love to travel, I have a sinking fund just for this. No regrets there – remember, you can budget for filet mignon or ramen noodles, friends. That's my filet mignon, and we've had, and continue to have, some phenomenal experiences because of this. You'll have your own categories and goals for sinking funds if you choose to do things this way, but one that is worth a special mention – and its own section entirely – is dedicated to cars and how we got rid of car payments for good.

ELIMINATING THE CAR PAYMENTS

Cash flowing your cars could really have a book devoted just to this idea. This may not be for everyone but now that I'm done with car payments, I don't foresee ever getting another car payment again. As noted in Chapter 2, if you have a car or lease payment, that goes into your listing of debts. You can then potentially tackle this by paying it off when you get to that particular debt. But what worked (incredibly) well for us was 'downgrading' both of our cars. We ended up calculating what our lease payouts would be – plus any mileage charges where we'd gone over the allotted annual mileage (that one can be painful) – and added that to our debt listing. We then paid these off in the order of our debts. Note that you may incur 'loyalty penalties,' which are a really sneaky way of having you roll your current lease into a newer and shinier one when the lease is up, or getting penalized financially if you don't. As noted in the prior chapter, we made the tough decision (tougher for him, no question) to trade in our Harley Davidson. We negotiated hard for the top of the *Kelley Blue Book* trade-in value, then added a couple thousand dollars we'd saved for this on top to trade for what was the first-ever paid for vehicle I'd ever owned.

It was amusing to see how much it seemed to throw the salesman off balance a bit when we had no need to talk to the financing department (they often make a good amount of money in this area). It helps to really research makes and models here for ratings, and you'll often find that a slightly older but very reputable car manufacturer is worth the same price you'd be paying for a newer, but less quality brand. A new car's value drops tremendously the moment it's driven off the lot, so a couple years old is the sweet spot here. As you likely know, your mechanic can help you with this decision and look over a vehicle you're considering buying to ensure it is sound. Most have a special discounted rate for this kind of thing; because I've been lucky to find a great mechanic that now takes care of all of our cars, he even did this for free.

Once we did this, we immediately started putting what had been our car payment into a savings account specifically for this every month so that we were basically paying ourselves for our next vehicle upgrade. That became our 'car sinking fund.'

To figure out how much you'll want to set aside for this fund, decide how long you'd like to keep your car and what your budget will be for your next upgrade, less the trade-in (or private sale) value of your current car. For example, in purposely simple numbers:

Current car's trade-in value: $4,000
Price point for next car: $10,000
Cash needed above trade-in: $6,000
Timeframe to the next car purchase: 24 months
Sinking fund: $6,000/24 months = $250/month

Plug in whatever numbers make sense for your personal situation that will allow you to keep paying off your debt (yours could be significantly higher or lower). This is obviously overly simple, not taking into account depreciation, current market conditions, the kind of vehicle you're looking to buy, interest rates, etc., but this should give you a sense of how to calculate what to put into your car's sinking fund. Using this example, you'll be ready to upgrade your car in 24 months once again, but this time **without a payment**. Then you'll start the process all over again at that point with whatever your *next* car upgrade budget is, and so on. And just like that, you will be officially done carrying a car payment.

Hear me out. The first time I heard of someone paying cash for their car, I immediately thought at first that it was both ridiculous and unattainable. Who does that? And *how*? So I wrote the idea off entirely, assuming it would only be possible if the car was a beater. A hoopty. You know, not a nice car. But depending on how motivated you are, you might want to seriously consider this, and the quality of the cars will continually get better because of your sinking funds. And please trust me when I say, if you have even a modicum of a competitive spirit, you will start competing with your partner and/or yourself about just *how* debt-free you can get, and how quickly. This is one hell of a way to knock out some debt.

I realize that this one may be slightly harder to wrap your head around if you're someone who takes pride in what you drive, and a good majority of us are. But here is a great place where long-term goals trump short-term inconveniences. Additionally, it's always an option to retrofit a backup camera, a sound or satellite map system, and even heated seats (who knew?). There are also aftermarket warranties that proved very beneficial in our case, saving us thousands of dollars for one of our vehicles despite my initial skepticism in this area. In full transparency, I liked (but did not love) what I think of as my level one cash-flowed car, level two was better, but I can honestly say that I absolutely love my now-level three car. Part of this is that it's newer and nicer overall, but mostly because she is so beautifully paid for. So. Paid. For. And *that* was well worth the first couple of years in the first two. Also worth mentioning...I am so looking forward to my next upgrade because they just keep getting better.

CHAPTER TEN

DEALING WITH SETBACKS

I felt a short chapter was needed to talk about any setbacks that may come up along the way. Honorable mention, if you will. Much like with anything else, sometimes the universe really does test your resolve once you've made a decision to move in a certain direction in your life. I won't call it Murphy's Law where if anything can go wrong it will necessarily, but more like the universe is almost testing you to see if you're *really sure* that this is what you want to do. It absolutely did for us back then – especially when we first got started.

Not long after finally getting all of this underway – truly, what felt like five minutes after calculating our total debt for the very first time and absorbing the magnitude of *that* number – the boiler broke, to the tune of $8,045. Come on, seriously? *Seriously* with this bullshit? And as I'm sure you well know, that is just not an optional feature of home ownership when you live with other people, my friends. Unfortunately, that well exceeded the $1,000 emergency fund we'd set aside when we started getting out of debt, so we had no choice but to finance it. But that loan immediately went into the debt listing in order and was eventually knocked out in time like all the other ones. There were also lulls in work and temporary declines in income during this time because of contract work, unexpected car repairs, etc., but we held firm to the process and just put our heads down and kept going. It paid off.

Fear of missing out (FOMO) also really factored in here. They say that what you focus on, you'll start seeing everywhere. Whatever the reason, I remember feeling that the moment I made the choice to stop spending frivolously, I wanted to buy everything. Every single damn thing. Maybe it's because even as an adult, I still hate being told what to do but in this case, *I* was the one denying *myself* these things in favor of a much bigger goal. Whatever the reason, I was fighting this ridiculous internal battle with myself and it brought out this incredibly juvenile feeling that 'everyone else was getting to do all these great big things' that made me just...irritable. I really had to confront this absurd line of thinking, then make the mental adjustment it took to realize that what we were doing really was for the better overall. My ex had the patience of a saint.

Why am I admitting to something so foolish and unflattering? Because as I hope I've made clear so far, my goal is to be as transparent as I can to hopefully spare *you* some of the pain of this learning curve. This process really does confront some very long-held beliefs and behaviors surrounding money that come from a billion different places inside. Unexamined, they shape – often very subconsciously – our behaviors and thoughts surrounding money that most people never get around to questioning. So we go along, blindly repeating the patterns (and often, mistakes) of past generations because we never learned any differently. We grew up simply assuming this was normal.

It's also worth mentioning here that all of this work you're going to be doing – that you've already *started* doing simply by reading this book up until this point – is really a pretty damn profound gift to your future self and your future generations depending on what you do with what you learn. You may rebel against even yourself so that you don't 'miss out' on all the great things your friends seem to be doing/buying/wearing, but you'll be focusing on long-term goals and successes that you're building in your own life with these short-term sacrifices. I can assure you, it will pay dividends down the road in some profound and even intangible ways.

CHAPTER ELEVEN

MENTAL ADJUSTMENTS

I n addition to the myriad ways we found to save money in our budget now that we finally had one, there were a lot of mental adjustments I had to make that really deserve their own chapter. Throughout this process, you're truly changing your relationship with money and perhaps for the first time, starting to confront some of the reasons you learned to do the things that led you here. Which is not to say any of them are good or bad – it just helps to understand why you do the things you do.

EMERGENCY FUNDS

As noted in Chapter 9, once you've done your budget and calculated your firehose, it's crucial that you set money aside for emergencies. But I also include this in the 'mental adjustment' chapter because it really did take some time for me to wrap my head around the logic this entails. Back then, we owed so much money to so many different people, yet we had 'savings' in various places that were paying us very little in interest. Instead of paying off some of that debt with those savings, we were paying obscene amounts of interest and finance charges to the companies we owed money to just for the privilege of having a loan with them. How on earth does that make sense? So while it took a little while to get to this point, we eventually decided to drop all of our savings down to *only* that $1,000 emergency fund and throw the rest at our debt. This was deeply uncomfortable for me because it removed what I had long thought of as my 'safety net,' but in doing so, we took out a large chunk of debt with everything else that we had in savings at the time.

This was a very scary, exhilarating, and *intentional* decision that we made after calculating exactly how much we could shorten the length of time it would take to get out of debt by doing this. It was an aggressive choice that removed a false layer of security that I know I had, and it forced me to be more aggressive about becoming debt-free. I have never regretted that decision. If your timeline is very long or your circumstances don't allow – again, seek financial advice. This is what worked for me, and the discomfort that came from removing that false sense of security put my motivation level on steroids to get the debt gone so these savings could resume. It helped *tremendously*.

A huge tip to file under mental adjustments: every time you go to make an impulse buy for anything at all but *don't* (high five!), immediately open your bank app and put exactly that amount that you were about to spend on your smallest debt. Immediately. Don't protest that you don't have it – you were just about to spend it so yes you do! There is something about the mental shift from indulgence to really stepping up your debt-free game that is very motivating. Truly – whether it was $10 or $500 doesn't matter. It's about the behavior you're changing and building momentum, which is huge. I'm telling you, this is how you get out of debt. Just keep chipping away at it and don't stop. Also, give yourself a 'cooling off' period of 1-14 days for a purchase that wasn't planned to make sure you really need it. Repeat after me: a hot tub is not an impulse buy (why are these even at festivals?!). Ever.

We should also talk about needs versus wants here. Yes, I know, this is kindergarten stuff, but bear with me for a minute because I think this is important to call out. When it comes to spending money, it helps to be very intentional about asking yourself which of these categories something falls into. You'll find that when you start this process, your motivation is at its highest (think New Year's diet resolutions – haha diet analogy even *here* for the win!) and all those little money wins you find will continue to fan this flame. It's easier at the beginning to cut out some of these extra 'wants' because there is so much low-hanging fruit when you first start out. But depending on how much debt you have to lose (here too! *Yes!* I know, I know, but if you only knew how easily amused I am), you may find – as I did – that there is a period when you are at the base of your biggest and final debt that you really just do. Not. Want. To. Deal. With. This. Process. Any. More. I had to spend a lot of time 'embracing the suck' and fighting the urge to just spend money however I wanted because it honestly felt like we'd never get there (so why bother, right?). I am here to tell you – if you don't stop, you *will* get there and it is so worth it. And this is where the mental adjustments come into play.

I'll say it again – I don't know who needs to hear this, but just because you can afford the payments doesn't mean you can afford something. There's also a vast difference between being cheap and being frugal – I want to make that clear. You can choose to spend like a baller once you're out of debt. Hell, that can be part of your budget *now* while you're in debt – it's all about how quickly you want to knock the debt out of your life, and what you want your financial future to look like. You're the one driving, my friend, so drive fast and use the guardrails or inch along in the slow lane like a happy little Sunday driver. Whatever fits your life the best.

If you haven't already, now's a good time to suggest that you pull your credit report from one of the three credit bureaus. You should be able to do this once a year for free (search this online), and it's a good idea to check periodically to be sure there's no fraudulent activity on your account. You can also sign up for an app that allows you to keep an eye on your credit score. Dispute anything on your credit report that looks to be inaccurate.

Here's a mental adjustment you may not like but I know someone out there needs to hear this: cut up your credit cards. Right now. Today. At the very least (yes, this sounds crazy but stay with me for the moment), maybe keep one and put it in a baggie full of water and freeze it. Yes, I'm serious. This way, you can still have access to it for emergencies, but you have to wait for the ice to thaw so you will have time to consider if the expense is absolutely necessary. The goal here is to teach yourself not to spend money you don't have. Think about the fact that our grandparents didn't even have credit cards. They simply had to pay for things, and if they couldn't, then they wouldn't get those things. Credit cards weren't even invented until 1949 by a man named Frank McNamara who created the 'Diners Club' card, and they're now a regular part of most of our lives.

For years when I couldn't afford...well, anything, really, I would use my credit card for anything above what I had in my checking account (even and especially for groceries). I'd pay the minimum balance each month along with an obscene amount of interest and then once a year (yes, a *year*), I would pay it off when I got my tax return. Guys, that is no fucking way to live. I was always an inch from poverty but felt like there wasn't much I could do about it, so I simply lived that way. I can't tell you how many times – and I actually get choked up when I remember how this felt – I had to put away groceries that were already on the belt because I couldn't afford the total. Do you know how much that sucks, and how humiliating it was to pretend I just didn't 'need' those two (or 20) things after all that day? This may or may not resonate with you but if it does on any level, I'd like you to know that you don't have to live like that anymore.

Another big mental adjustment that took some time to both wrap my head around and then actually do, was to lower my 401(k) contribution from the maximum yearly contribution allowed to a significantly lower amount to free up money for that 'extra' each month to pay off debt. This is going to come with strong opinions and this is absolutely not financial advice – none of this is, and I'd again encourage you to speak to a financial advisor for your specific situation. But I decided to lower my monthly contribution down to the amount that my company matched at the time so that I wasn't leaving money on the table. I only did this for a *very finite* period of time in order to pay off debt more quickly with the money it freed up each paycheck because we were almost there. But damn, that was uncomfortable and further fueled that motivation level, too.

It's also important to get on the same page if doing this with a partner. If you're not, see if you can find an accountability partner to bounce some of these ideas and challenges off of. Develop a 'team' of people you spend the most time with who can pull you forward – a financial planner, insurance agent, accountant, people you admire in business who can mentor you, people who really have their financial shit together and/or are successful in their chosen careers, etc. – whatever that looks like for you. Remember, you don't get a financial planner when you are wealthy. You get one to help you *become* wealthy, just like you get your life insurance when you're healthy. All of these things are meant to help you build a strong financial foundation and scaffolding for your life.

Being in debt up until that point in my life really had become my 'mental wallpaper' – that $98,000 in student loans I'd been carrying for the last decade and a half were something I just begrudgingly accepted as part of my life. But it really doesn't have to be the norm at all anymore. Try to reframe that you're not someone *getting out of debt*, you're becoming someone who simply *no longer borrows or carries debt.* And if you keep going, you *will* become someone who is debt-free. See the difference? It's a very subtle, but profound, mental shift.

CHAPTER TWELVE

NEXT STEPS

S o here, my friends, is where it gets good. And I mean *good*. I'm grateful to you for sticking with me through all this craziness, and by this point we've covered a ton of information. And here you are, still reading. High freaking five to you (seriously)! I hope that at least some of this resonated with you enough to make you realize that getting out of debt might be worth considering, and I sincerely hope you have fully internalized that it *is* possible. You may have even gotten started and weighed out your debt so you know exactly where you stand (Chapter 2), then created a budget to determine the 'firehose' payment you'll use to pay off that debt (Chapter 3). I don't doubt that you've already started to find some creative ways to maximize that firehose, too (Chapters 4, 5, 6, 7, and 8).

Hopefully, you've created your $1,000 emergency fund as well as some sinking funds (Chapter 9) that are specific to your goals. You have dealt with the various things that life throws at you, if necessary (Chapter 10). I hope you've also started building a team to cheer you on and help you reach your financial goals (Chapter 11) – this again may include an independent insurance agent, a financial planner, and at least one accountability partner to keep you on track and cheer you on with every one of the wins you'll be making happen along the way. And perhaps *most* importantly – you've *stopped borrowing money* because of that initial emergency fund (Chapters 9 and 11, with the amount depending on your personal circumstances).

The single best piece of advice I can give you to sum up this book would be to just keep going and *do not stop*. You'll want to (ohh, how badly I wanted to), you'll be tempted to say screw this because it's taking too long, you'll be tempted to indulge in purchases that throw all of your hard work out the window....but don't. You *can* do this.

I fought so many unexpected demons during this process and it forced me to really confront a lot of things that I grew up with that didn't feel good at all. I wished vehemently that I had someone to properly teach me all of this back then so that I could do it right from the beginning. But you know what? I didn't, and even if I *was* lucky enough to have had someone, I may not have been ready to hear any of it anyways. I needed to go through every single thing I went through to become who I am today.

Somewhere along the way, I started keeping a journal of all these little lessons, stumbling blocks, dollar amounts, wins – all of it – and that eventually became the book you're reading today. We all know the best time to plant a tree was twenty years ago but the second-best time – and the only one that any of us really have – is *today*. So get started, my friend. I promise you'll be glad you did, and you're welcome to hold me to that.

You'll realize that you can do anything all – but that doesn't mean that you can do everything. You'll make choices about the things that matter most to you and you're going to confront where some of your beliefs and patterns with money came from. But you're essentially setting these limits to live a limitless life. Wealth is a state of mind and I now understand it to be comfort in your own skin, financially. I have never in my life been this comfortable handling money even though I realize there is always more to continue learning, and I am.

I also understand now that retirement is a dollar figure, not an age. Some people retire at age 65 because they turned 65. Some of us retire when our union or pension dictates. Some can't retire until much, much later because we cannot afford to stop working. And still some of us retire at a much younger age simply because we *can*.

That's the goal, friends – to get to that financial milestone that will allow you to maintain the lifestyle you'd like to maintain in retirement. Then you get to decide what you'll do for the next chapter of your life by *choice* and not out of financial necessity. Mine will involve a boat and a lot of time on the water, I can assure you.

All of this has allowed me to make much bolder career decisions, and has led to some incredible connections with people in talking about this process. Most important for me, though, has been how positively it's impacted the way I teach my sons to handle money. This really is a beautiful legacy to leave your kids. Since nobody talked to me about money growing up, I now speak openly, freely, and often with my sons and their girlfriends about all of this. I teach them what I've learned and then let them make their own decisions from that point on.

In some of those car upgrades, we used to have them research the *Kelley Blue Book* value of our cars to understand how that all works. Then we'd have them sit at the table with the dealerships and private party sellers with us to be part of the negotiation process. They each opened Roth IRAs when they turned 18 to get a head start on the absolute beauty of compound interest, and we're lucky to have a phenomenal financial advisor who has turned into a friend (we're due for dinner, by the way, Rob).

I talk about these things to the point that my sons (jokingly of course) threaten dire consequences if they have to hear the word 'budget' one more time – but my friends, they *are* listening. How do I know this? My older son was recently talking to his girlfriend in the kitchen about a trip to Nashville they were planning since both had always wanted to go there. He casually mentioned to her that if they start a sinking fund for this, they'd be able to do that trip in a couple months and cash flow it. Ohhhh, my heart! They *are* listening, and they absolutely do follow in the example you are showing them in the way you live your own life.

Can we also talk about generosity for a moment? I heard someone say recently the profoundly simple phrase, 'givers get.' What a beautiful way to put it – I have always believed this. Some of the best people I know are also the ones that are the most (quietly) generous in so many different ways – with their time, their heart, and their wallet.

One of my favorite things to do – and it's so small – is to pay for the car behind me in line. Tip obscenely well, but make sure they don't know about it until you've left. Hell, tip the entire bill amount if you can. Or even better – pay for another table as you leave. Buy candy for the cashier that's having a rough day. Drop off food to your local police or fire station to thank them for their service (truly, thank the hell out of them for their service regardless of whether you buy them food).

It doesn't matter what you do and it's most certainly not about any crazy dollar amount – but it's worth noting that some sort of shift happens when you start getting more and more generous with money as you're able, and you're no longer living paycheck to paycheck. The positive ripple effect it causes will unfold in so many beautiful ways in your life – something made so much more possible by being fully debt-free.

I firmly believe that you'll never regret generosity, particularly when you do it from a place of gratitude for all the blessings in your own life. And it almost seems to pave the way for even greater good fortune – I don't fully know how to explain it, but I do know that it does. Life is *good*, my friends, even when it's hard. So damn good.

CHAPTER THIRTEEN

DEBT FREEDOM

After beginning this crazy journey on September 14, 2017, my then-husband and I became fully, 100%, owe-no-one-a-damn-thing debt-free on December 19, 2022. It took 5 years, 3 months, and 5 days (but who's counting, right?), and we paid off $177,479 – that's *one hundred, seventy-seven thousand, four hundred and seventy-nine dollars* – worth of debt, *plus* the house on top of that mountain of debt. As difficult as it was at times, it was worth every single thing we went through to get here. Every single thing, even the especially challenging parts when giving up just felt like it would have been so much easier.

When it started to become real that we were most definitely *going* to hit that finish line, we started thinking about some really incredible ways to mark this occasion and celebrate the hell out of this. At some point during the dumpster fire that was COVID, one of my favorite musicians that we'd seen do live shows a couple of time started doing house concerts. When I saw this, I knew in that moment that this was how we were going to celebrate becoming debt-free.

So without telling any of them why, we chose just a handful of our friends that in one way or another were part of this debt-free journey (whether they realized it or not) and we had one *hell* of a house party with the exceptionally talented – and more importantly, so kind – Sean Rowe (https://www.seanrowe.net). Sean gave me his permission to share his name here when I finally (finally!) got to the finish line of writing this book (thank you for everything, my friend, and we're due for our next dinner, too). We announced to our friends over a pretty damn memorable toast exactly why they were all there with us that night. That experience and that connection with every single person in the room that night will always remain one of those pinnacle moments you just simply never forget. Some of our friends knew well what we were going through the last five years, my sons obviously knew very well, but some that came that night had no idea. I can assure you, though, all of them had questions afterwards. It really helped fuel my desire to write this book. That night and honestly, this whole process, was nothing shy of amazing and I swear to you, it just keeps getting better.

This is simply how I live now – I use sinking funds for a handful of things that are important to me including that travel fund I mentioned, as well as a few for things like cars, insurance, and gifts so there are never any surprises there. I even use them sometimes for shorter-term purchases that aren't easily cash-flowed, such as my son's upcoming college graduation party. I had an amusing conversation with my bank recently about why I had so many separate little savings accounts – apparently sinking funds aren't that common. For that matter, being debt-free is not that common either. Debt is very much a societal norm, and not all debt is 'bad' or unnecessary.

It's also worth noting that as we all know, life throws you curveballs and sometimes, this requires needing to regroup with your finances. Personally, I've shifted to now doing this on my own. I will be forever grateful to my ex for all that we went through together and for weathering all the storms that this brought up for me (which, thankfully, we can still joke about now). Just know that if you ever do have to go back into debt for whatever reason, you know how to do this. In fact, you can't *unknow* it; this process will forever inform your spending patterns and behavior going forward. It kind of ruins you for spending like a jerk, if I'm being honest. Put whatever your debt is back in line, re-tighten your budget and your belt, and get back on the scale until you're where you want to be again. Repeat as many times as necessary, and don't forget to continue having budget check-ins regularly to look at where you are to be sure your income and outgo are both where you want them to be.

Remember when we spoke about that initial emergency fund in Chapter 9? Once you hit your own personal finish line and pay off your own debt, I'd strongly recommend you set aside at least four months of expenses (ideally six at minimum) to really give yourself a safety net. Since you've already done your budget and tweaked it along the way as your debt gets smaller, you already know exactly what your expenses are to the dollar. Set aside several months' worth of this amount to get to a point where you truly cushion yourself from potentially ever having to borrow money again, should your income change.

Some people have very strong opinions about paying off your house, depending on your interest rate, etc. I am most certainly not here to argue – there *are* some worthwhile conversations to be had there. But here's what I know, for *me*. I don't like having any sort of debt in my life anymore now that I know intimately what being debt-free feels like. So that's what I choose to continually work at in my own life. I also realize there are all kinds of points and rewards and trinkets for various credit cards, etc. – again, no judgment or strong opinions from me for you and what you do. I just know what has worked beautifully for me and I want you to fully understand how to pay off all of your debt, should you decide that's what makes sense in your life.

At the time of finishing this book, I've begun speaking to businesses to teach their employees – particularly those in higher income brackets – how to maximize their income to get out of debt. This is something I love doing because I've met people who make well into six figures who save nothing at all (but have tons of shiny toys with large payments on them), as well as people who are barely getting by but who are amazing at staying out of debt and finding ways to save money. Guys, it has almost *nothing* to do with what your income level is but everything to do with what you *do* with it, and with understanding your mindset that ultimately determines how you handle money. I'm also putting together an updated class to teach money handling to young adults in particular in order to share some of the lessons I wish someone gave me back then. And I speak on becoming debt-free. It is my sincere hope that you have at least questioned some of your own long-held beliefs about debt and money, and that you decide to make even tiny, incremental changes in your life to improve both.

Also at the time of this writing, both of my young adult sons are finishing college and both have gotten through completely debt-free. I am ridiculously proud of both of them for the way they handle money, which I really believe comes from several years now of talking about this intentionally and openly in our household. Please don't misunderstand – I am not taking credit for how well they do in this area, not at all. They very much make their own decisions, some of which I agree with, while some may differ on how I would do things. What I am most proud of is that they are *intentional* about their decisions and the financial ramifications for each of them.

College is a perfect example: after looking at the financial packages for various away schools, they both looked at what the entire four-year tuition and living on campus would cost. We discussed the amount we were able to contribute for them, as well as how much they'd have in student loans to bridge the difference when they graduated (the total of which far exceeded any potential initial salaries they anticipated). One chose community college for the first two years and a local college for the remaining two for his bachelor's degree, and the other chose a business school that was not only affordable but helped him launch his own business.

Affording college or choosing a trade is well worth its own book entirely because there are so, so many great paths for kids after high school (many of which may have nothing whatsoever to do with college at all and everything to do with that particular young adult). Suffice it to say, I am a firm believer in finding what's best for them and cheering for them along the way. Automatically assuming an expensive education that saddles them (or their parents) with a mountain of student loan debt is not something I am a fan of from my own personal experience there. Of course, there are fields and degrees that simply require that but for the rest...you get the idea.

It's worth noting that I no longer avoid my mailbox as a means of 'budgeting' – partly because most of my bills are electronically delivered and no one mails anything fun anymore anyways (other than my neighbor, of course) – but mostly because I am in a much more stable and comfortable place with money than I have ever been before. This has less to do with my income and everything to do with the fact that I not only know what I'm making, but I know exactly what I'm spending and I make very intentional choices about this. Holidays and birthdays no longer surprise me when it comes to budgeting these out – they come at the same time every year. Who knew?

Speaking of electronic bills – I also no longer let any utilities or service providers automatically 'pull' my monthly payment after getting absolutely socked with a $2,300+ utility bill from a very poorly handled electric company. I learned that day that had I allowed them to 'pull' this amount automatically versus my manually pushing it out to them, they would have depleted my checking account in one fell swoop. And I would have been the one responsible for all the overdraft charges for everything else pending with my bank. Be careful here and be sure that *you* are the one pushing out your monthly bill payments.

It's also worth noting that now when I get a raise, I don't adjust my standard of living or budget at all. I set up an automatic transfer for whatever the increase is so that it goes straight into a high-yield savings or investment account. I don't even feel the difference so I don't miss it *and* I get to reap the beautiful power of compound interest. I try to live beneath my means in this way and not spend frivolously just because I can.

But that said, I also believe you get what you pay for. I remember hearing something years ago that for the life of me, cannot remember who to quote. It went something like, 'Don't cheap out on things that separate your ass from the ground' – meaning, things like tires, shoes, a mattress, good sheets, etc. While I paraphrased quite elegantly here (I mean, obviously), hopefully you get the idea. I've come to really believe in this – quality does matter, and some things are worth being a little more spendy on than others. I'll add food to this list, too, since food is medicine, after all.

Do you remember way back in Chapter 1 when I mentioned how great it would be not to have to look at the price tag for something you wanted to buy? I realized not that long ago after leaving a store that I had never even looked at the total when I paid – couldn't even have guessed what my total had been – and I felt this unexpected wave of emotion because it occurred to me in that moment that *I made it*. I broke the mold of my own childhood, raising young men I *know* damn well that I'm proud of who are living so differently than I ever thought possible back then. And I'm going to keep sharing what I've learned with anyone who needs (and more importantly, wants) to hear this.

I sincerely hope you get to your own personal goal line, whatever that may be, and I *really* hope you get to feel that same feeling that I did once you suddenly realize that *you've* arrived (whatever that looks like, for you). Getting out of debt really is as simple as I've laid out here, and yet it's as complex as each of us are. Create and monitor your budget. Recognize where your money is going and get control over that. Save so you no longer have to borrow. Pay it all off. And once you've got all of *that* under control, be sure you're investing in your future (that's another book entirely). People who don't save any money, don't have any money saved, right? Live on less than you make. Be as generous as your heart desires and your wallet allows. All of this will eventually change your mindset and your relationship with money for the better, and in ways you've never imagined. And always remember, life is *good*, and it just keeps getting better. Never lose sight of your goals, dream so much bigger than you ever thought possible, get started, and do not stop. *You've got this!*

CHAPTER FOURTEEN

THE BONUS CHAPTER: REAL PEOPLE SHARING THEIR BEST TIPS

N ow that you've heard a whole lot more than you may have ever wanted to from (and about) me, I want you to hear some advice from other real people who were willing to share their own best tips, life lessons, personal struggles, and just solid money handling advice. I absolutely love having these 'taboo' money conversations and hearing how other people do this, and I am especially grateful to each of them for being willing to speak so candidly about money when so few normally are. Note that these views are strictly their own and may align with my own perfectly or perhaps not at all, some are amusing and some are very personal, but there isn't a single one that I didn't learn something from. So without further ado, here they are in their own words in no particular order (edited only for clarity and only if needed), again with my immense gratitude to all of you!

Kristen Leigh (SC):

I'm a big fan of YNAB [the You Need a Budget app], which uses zero-based budgeting. This app has been a gamechanger for me. Coupled with the profit-first methodology (profit-first uses percentages to allocate funds to profit/owner's pay/taxes/operating expenses with every inflow; the percentages vary depending on each business), it's helped me manage my small business finances also. I cannot even believe the difference in how I can save and invest now. I believe so strongly in the product that I became a certified coach and now exclusively help human trafficking survivors in my area handle their money (for many of them this is the first time they've had access to their *own* money). I opted not to continue being a paid budgeting coach. I just volunteer these services to "pay it forward."

I also encourage women to get educated in finances! There are some great (even free) resources out there. I try to share with as many as I can about reading *The Simple Path to Wealth* and *I Will Teach You To Be Rich* (and others). I'm a big fan of Fidelity and their services for Roth IRAs/t-IRAs/HSAs/SEP-IRAs/etc., and now even their cash management accounts (CMAs) which function like checking accounts but with much better features. All of these can be managed on your phone via their app! So it makes these services more accessible than ever before by *anyone.*

I hesitate to share my exact percentages as everything is sooo dependent on your tax bracket, your expenses, etc. My scenario is unique. Every business is. A CPA may need to be consulted to ensure taxes especially are properly covered.

Shelley Williams (Washington):

If you are married or in a committed relationship, you need to know about your finances. I see too many people not being involved and have no idea where money is spent or what the bills are. If your partner wants to keep it a secret and not let you know, that's a huge red flag! I have seen too many people bury their head in the sand and have a big surprise that money they thought they were saving together had been spent. You need to watch out for your own financial security. Always make sure you have a bank account and a credit card in your own name so you have it to fall back on if you need it. Also, know where bank accounts, account numbers, and passwords are. It's really hard if someone passes away and the other person handled everything, and they have no idea where to start – especially when you are grieving and struggling. It will make life a little easier.

Jarrett Hobbs (Henrietta, NY):

I think it's important to leverage company benefits. Sign up for rewards (credit cards, hotels, gas cards, etc.). Rental car tip: Look at the rental car site for discounts. It's cheaper to rent for five days than four days. Rent the extra day and save!

Stephanie D. (South Carolina):

Meal plan to save on groceries. Have a budget, track your spending. It's never too late to save. Everyone should have an old car. Who are the Joneses? Keeping up with them is no longer relevant. Relocate to a low cost of living area.

Julie Sulli (Charlotte, NC):

Don't lend money that you can't afford not to get back. Do not make plans to spend that money, or any other money that is owed to you, but not in your physical possession. Things don't always go as planned and spending money that you thought you'd have will cause disappointment and can leave you in a bad situation.

Also, don't make only enough money to just get by. Even if you only make a little more than what you need for your necessities, having even a little extra each week to save will reduce a lot of stress.

Carol Greene (West Henrietta, NY):

First, call your credit card companies and see if you can negotiate a lower percentage on the card(s). Then start to pay off the smallest credit card first. Then take that payment and add it to the next credit card until you get to the highest one and pay that. The payoff should be quicker this way.

Gin Stephens (Surfside Beach, SC):

Learn to cook and eat at home. In the current 'Door Dash' and convenience foods environment, you can save a great deal of money that way. Buy a basic cookbook or find recipes you love online and start there, working through the recipes and honing your skills. Buy staples such as rice and beans in bulk, and experiment with the flavors you love. Or consider a meal planning app such as eMeals, which allows you to choose your weekly recipes and creates a shopping list for you, right in the app. You'll be amazed at what you create and how much money you save!

Donna Campo (Louisiana):

About five years into our 30-year mortgage, I started downloading the amortization chart every month and I would look at how much the last payment was and the scheduled date. I would send in extra payments trying to knock that last payment out. That was always my goal. Seeing that last date move up is so rewarding. We paid off our 30-year mortgage in 12 years. I also tracked our net worth so that the extra payments did not hurt that overall number as we were reducing debt and increasing equity at the same time. It was like paying ourselves. Retired at 55, downsized and living debt-free.

Mike B. (Penfield, NY):

Turn off all access to Amazon (and all shopping sites) after 11 pm.

Sarah Johnson (Pittsford, NY):

Ok, maybe a money tip you already have but I have the cheat code to free money. Pay for everything possible with a credit card instead of cash. Then pay off said card weekly instead of monthly to avoid any interest fees. You have to be thoughtful of your purchases and make sure the money in the bank can cover the totals weekly though.

I have five credit cards and switch around depending on the deals each has. I've earned thousands of dollars in free clothing and products this way using the points. I haven't saved up enough points for a trip or anything, but back to school shopping and Christmas presents do get purchased with points money.

Jeff Carlucci (Greece, NY):

Intuitively, people want to try to pay down the debt with the highest interest rate. Why are our brains wired this way? In anything in life, we don't try to do the hardest thing first. When you get a new video game, you don't put it on hardest mode and work your way down to easiest, right? If you're trying to teach your six-year-old how to bowl, would you give her a 15-lb ball with no gutter bumpers and expect her to bowl a great game? Would you try to climb Mount Everest without climbing smaller peaks first? Start small, start easy, start smart, and slowly build up. The key is to start! There's a thrill that comes with paying off that first debt – it might be small but it's a *big* win!

James Johnson (Los Angeles, CA):

Measure every single thing you're spending for three months and track every single dollar that comes in. Working in the data field, I find that you can't measure any type of progress without establishing a baseline first. This is why I always recommend tracking every single purchase you make, even if it is just $1, for 60 to 90 days. Carry a small notebook around with you, or use a note app on your smart phone. Many people often don't realize where their money is really going. Once a financial baseline is determined, it is possible to then set a budget and plan your finances more appropriately to allow you to get out of debt.

Tim Berl (Henrietta, NY):

Best financial advice I ever received came from my father. Pay yourself first! Retirement investment is critical from Day One and stick to it...pay yourself first!

Tammie H. (Ridgefield, Washington):

When you start a new job, take the employer's match for retirement if applicable. If the employer's match is 3%, right away sign up for the matching 3% so you won't ever miss it - especially if you were like me and in your 40s with no retirement. Every year since then, I bumped up my percentages until I'm now at 16%.

I found myself at the age of 47 divorced, with no retirement, and thinking to myself I have 15 years to work and what am I going to live on? And I realized that there are so many other women in the same age group in the same situation. My children are raised. I was on my own and realized I had no one but myself to count on and I was never going to count on a man again – it was up to me to take care of myself. I used the above recommendation that I received from somebody else and that's how I started on my path to retirement for myself. Now here I am, 12 years later, still alone by choice, with $650,000 in my retirement fund. I realize it's not enough yet according to my financial advisor, but I'm still fucking proud of what I've done in 12 years. I know that if I can do it, so can other women in the same situation.

Melissa Day (Buffalo, NY):

Do not use credit cards under any circumstances if you can't afford to pay off the balance *in full* when you use it. Do not use a *payday lender* loan. Do not consolidate your student loans when the interest rates are high.

Derek Carstairs (Rochester, NY):

My advice is, don't ever ask me for financial advice.

Anonymous (Tennessee):

My in-laws sat us down at the beginning and really helped us start out right. We did the Dave Ramsey method, except we never stopped saving for retirement. We put 10% of our income into a separate bank fund and it is where our church donations come from, as well as donations to dog rescues, buying gas for strangers, groceries at the end of the month for someone at Kroger, library fines, overextended hot lunch tabs, etc. My husband refers to it as 'giving grants from the foundation.'

Jim Greene (West Henrietta, NY):

Making an extra payment on your mortgage once a year knocks your 30-year mortgage down to 21 years (using the total monthly payment – principal, escrow, and interest).

Jim VanBrederode (Gates, NY):

The day your child is born, go open a NYS College 529 savings plan. This was the best advice someone gave to me and I was able to send my two children to state schools with no loans! Contributing to the fund over 18 years was painless and small but the payout was was huge when it was college time!

Betsy H. (Vancouver, WA):

'Interest is the price you pay when you want something now,' was what my college economics professor had said. Unfortunately, after I graduated, got my first job, and my first credit card, I failed to remember that sage advice. I racked up close to $17,000 in debt, much of it because I could only afford to make the minimum monthly payment. Finally, struggling under the debt, I went crying to my mother for help. She graciously loaned me the money and drew up a payment schedule that included interest. I paid off the credit card and paid her back – every penny plus interest. My parents never discussed how to handle money. I learned the hard way. Moral of the story: parents, teach your children about money, credit, and investing from an early age. Every financial decision or transaction they make will have a corresponding consequence. Set them up for positive consequences!

Joanne Macek (Pittsford, NY):

I have another mortgage one! Step 1: Buy a house that doesn't make you "house poor." Banks (at least used to!) approve you for *way* more than you *should* borrow. Step 2: Look at the amount of principal you are paying and double it. Continue adding that to every payment! We paid ours off in about 1/2 the time! Also, if you *have to* take a car loan, keep that car for *way* longer than it takes you to pay off the loan. When the car is paid off, put the payment amount in a savings account and pay for your next vehicle in cash!

Kathy C. (Texas):

I wish my younger, newly married self could understand the true cost of debt (and interest!), and the true benefits of beginning to save early and the interest accrued.

Veronica VanBrederode (Gates, NY):

Open a deferred compensation plan the moment you get your first job. It will reduce your taxable income and help you build a sizable savings for retirement.

Sheri (Alabama):

I 100% wish I had known about financial abuse by a partner when I was in my first marriage. It wasn't until after we split and I started my recovery journey and I learned about it that I realized what was happening. If I had known way back then and had been aware of the signs, I could have saved so much stress and drama and wasted money.

Stacy Irwin Ristvedt (Concord, CA):

Do not get into a marriage or partnership with someone who is not fiscally aligned with you. If you cannot have the conversation to know where you stand, you are not ready (or it's not right).

Steve Winner (Rush, NY):

I've always been a bit conservative. Spend wisely, save wisely. Use a good financial advisor.

Helen Vanderlan (Irondequoit, NY):

Learn to cook, because ordering food costs money. And get travel cards! Make sure you can pay them off monthly then book some trips!

Anonymous:

Live below your means. Don't use credit cards for purchases you don't have the cash to pay off, and better off, don't use credit cards at all if you have bad money management or spending habits. Make sure to have a 6-month emergency fund since the job market is so unstable.

Tammi Flom (Minnesota):

We used Dave Ramsey as a guide. Best thing for me was documenting *all* outgoing money to actually see where we were spending and spending excessively to cut back. We learned we spent too much eating out, and started packing lunches and eating more meals at home. Documenting spending was an eye-opener to helping with a budget.

Lisa (Atlanta, GA):

I wish my 20-year-old self knew to invest at regular intervals into a low-cost index fund. "VTSAX and chill" (Vanguard Total Stock Market Index Fund). It's not rocket science. Just open an account and keep pumping money into it, then do nothing. So easy! Open a Roth IRA if you don't have a 401(k). Couples should have a monthly finance meeting to go over all accounts and set goals.

Anonymous:

Shop around for insurance each year. Super fast and an easy way to save a lot of money.

Diane Stocks Skeel (Arkansas):

100% Dave Ramsey!!! We just paid off our house after 24 years! We struggled for many years before someone invited us to a Dave Ramsey class!! It changed our lives!!!!

P.S. Why do we not make paying off a house a major party? No one I know ever talks about it. I know *no one* who's ever told me they paid their house off. I want to shout it out loud, but feel like it's inappropriate!! Why is that?!

Jaime Toth Barbee (Pennsylvania):

We are Dave Ramsey followers in Baby Step 7 and paid off our house in 2020 – you are absolutely right about the importance of paying off your house! It's a freedom like no other!

Sue Maduro (Henrietta, NY):

At one point in my life, I had $22k of credit card debt and went into a spiral realizing how deep in debt I was. I was making minimum payments on multiple cards, which was getting me nowhere fast. I learned about the debt snowball process and started applying it, and within 2-1/2 years it was paid off! It was wild making $700 payments to one card – if you think you can't ever do that (I thought so too), you *can!*

One of my favorite money tips is to keep separate accounts for specific funds so you don't have to wonder if you have enough money for specific purchases. If all your money is in one checking or savings account, it's hard to know what you have left after your bills. When you get paid, transfer set amounts of money into your designated accounts. Now you know your budget for that pay period! If you don't have enough saved in that account for something, wait until you do.

For example, I have individual accounts for a car fund (repairs, savings for a new car), home improvements (hiring contractors, home repairs/maintenance), living expenses (gas, subscriptions, hair stylist, minor miscellaneous purchases), food (groceries, restaurants), Christmas (gifts, shipping, decorations). I also have separate debit cards for each account with a picture that indicates what the card is for. The car fund has a car on it, my home improvements card has a house under construction, and my favorite (and most commented on) is my food card – it has fresh berries on it – so I know it's for food! Aside from that, only keep enough money in your general checking account for your monthly bills- designate the rest to your other accounts!

Jim Ringley (Tampa, FL):

Typically, banks will let you open several accounts. And particularly if you live paycheck to paycheck, open multiple accounts and assign them names (you can customize the names). Sometimes you have bills you only pay once every six months or once per year, so I'd open an annual account as well as a monthly bills account, then a savings account and maybe even a pocket change account. One of the things I've struggled with or that I've seen friends struggle with were the annual bills that come due and you forgot about them. Instead of being unprepared to pay that unexpected $3k all at once, take your biweekly check and automatically transfer that annual bill amount divided by 26, so you'll have this money ready to be go when that bill comes.

Then do the same monthly: take all your bills and determine the monthly amount. When your check comes, transfer whatever that amount is to the monthly bill account so it's all ready to go. The bank can even do this automatically, and then it's all right there ready to go in front of your face every time you log in to your bank. You can also use those amounts as a short-term loan for yourself, if you need to, as long as you put it back as soon as you're able to. And – if you're good in Excel, do your finances in an Excel document.

We put money into only one shared account that pays bills and accumulates for savings for house-related things. Otherwise, we keep finances separately.

The greatest thing I've ever done for myself is having a savings account, knowing I don't have to rely on anyone.

Kelly (Alberta, Canada):

I think that cars cause more money problems than anything else. I think one of the biggest reasons that we have been successful with money is that we haven't had a car payment in the last 25 years. We keep our vehicles for a long time (we had our last car for 18 years) and when we needed a new vehicle, we bought it with cash. If you don't have enough money to buy a vehicle with cash, that vehicle is too expensive for you.

Sue M. (Michigan):

My advice would be: Live within your budget. You might need to buy a used car instead of new. Don't carry a credit card balance. Buy only what you can afford. Learn to *save* money. Take good care of everything you own.

Bob Melville (Chili, NY):

How to get out of debt? Simple: Don't get into debt!!

Apart from mortgages on two homes and a car loan, we have never incurred other debt. Why? Interest paid on debt is like throwing money away! My tips after 40+ years of work and 10 years of retirement:

1– Live in housing you can afford! You don't need a McMansion if it consumes a large portion of your pay. Also, when buying a house, put as much down as you can afford. And get the shortest term – savings in interest over the life of 15-year versus 30-year loans is the equivalent of over ½ the original purchase price (!).

2– Pay cash for vehicles and buy only what you can afford. Ignore dealers' monthly payment pitches. Rather, look at the "out the door" price, and pay it in cash if at all possible. If you must finance, use the shortest term you can manage.

3– Live beneath your means! You don't need an expensive new car every couple of years. Pay cash for gently used 2 – 3-year-old cars then drive them until they wear out. Skip spendy vacations. And pay cash (don't incur debt on a credit card to pay for vacation).

4– Invest raises/bonuses. It's fine to spend a little on a celebratory dinner out, or perhaps a weekend getaway. But sock away the rest!

5– Begin saving early!! I started putting away money for the kids' education two years *before* our first child was born. Twenty-seven years later, I had put three kids through college – including two with master's degrees – with no student loans.

6- Likewise invest early in an IRA, or better yet in a Roth IRA. Even if you only put away 2% of your pay, over a 40-year career it will grow into an impressive pile of money.

7– Take full advantage of your employer's 401(k) and matching contributions if offered. If you cannot afford the maximum contribution, "start small" like perhaps a 2% salary contribution. Then as your income rises, increase your contribution percentage – at least until you max out the employer's contribution limit. (Your employer's contributions are "free" money. *And* they accumulate tax-free until after you retire.)

8– If you work/are paid for overtime, don't spend the extra cash! Save or invest your overtime pay or use it to pay down other debt.

9– Don't gamble! Gambling is 'tax on stupid people' (that's why it's pushed so hard by the state!). Skip the lottery, scratchers, casinos, etc.

Alexa Seefeldt (New Jersey):

Talk about money. Talk about it with your partner, with your parents, with your friends, with your coworkers. The more you talk about it, the more comfortable it becomes and you will learn from others.

Joy Hildreth Breedlove (Central Oregon):

We used the Dave Ramsey method to become debt-free. We also underspend our income so now at retirement, we have more money.

Nettie (Arizona):

Shop the ads for groceries and clip the digital coupons, then check your receipt before leaving the store to make sure the discounts come off. Often times they don't, and I've saved around $200 by checking receipts over the last year by going back to customer service to get the discount/refund. When a grocery item is on sale, buy as much as you can to stock up until it's on sale again next time. Also, *not* spending on things you don't need generates more wealth. It's taken us almost 20 years to save a year's worth of income for "just in case" and we finally did it! My husband got laid off last month after working for the same company for 19 years, and because of careful saving, we aren't panicking *yet*.

We've saved by using Cricket for cell service instead of Verizon, rarely eating out at fancy restaurants and using restaurant coupons for date nights, rarely going to the movies, and shopping clearance racks for next season (even for things likes sunscreen!). Our kids have much older-generation cell phones and have lived to tell the story, we drive fuel-efficient cars, and generally wait to buy something until it's on sale, if at all possible.

We get receipts for *everything* we spend, and every month I enter all spending into a spreadsheet to see where our money is going. It can be *very* eye-opening to see how fast the Polar Pops or Starbucks here and there adds up! Just makes you more conscious of your spending habits. Those are my main tips.

Leanne Carlson (Minnesota):

Always live within your means, and the only debt you should have is your mortgage, if any. Annually, look at different carriers for trash removal, insurance, internet, etc., to assess the competition because sneaky fees come into play or what not. If you still have the best deal around or don't want the hassle of switching, ask for a loyalty discount after a few years. When a child goes to college without a car, update your auto insurance. Always act as if you have a car payment, so there is cash for the next one. Pay yourself first. Max out your 401(k) and/or Roth IRA. Splurge every once in a while. Do not deprive yourself of vacations, they are just as fun taken on a budget!

Anonymous:

I'd like to add learn to be happy with what you have. I took out a $50k loan on a brand-new SUV back in 2022. All my friends and family looked at me in it and saw a 'successful' man. And it felt good pulling up to family gatherings and hearing my family talk and say things like, "Look at him in his new car." Meanwhile, my wallet was empty. Now I see people in their brand-new cars, and I feel sorry for them. I now drive a beat up 2017 Fusion... ask me if I'm happy? Hell yes! The extra cash we save, I get to save for my kids' college fund. We get to go out to the movies and all sorts of stuff. Biggest tip...learn to be happy with what you have because it's the people, not the stuff, that matters.

...

I am purposely choosing to end this book with that last one because I firmly believe that at the end of the day, it's only *ever* been about the people in our lives that truly matters. I will always credit my sister for teaching me to love my people out loud, and if you know me then you know that I will happily 'make it weird' without apologies. So to all the people in my tiny but happy little circle, and in particular those that have inspired me to write this book, thank you for *every damn good thing* you've all brought to my life. Happy debt-free journey, my friends!

Acknowledgements

While there are quite a few people that inspired me to write this book – my sons in particular – there are a few people I want to mention and thank here. One of the quotes in Chapter 14 may be by a name you recognize – Gin Stephens is the *New York Times* bestselling author of many books, including *Fast. Feast. Repeat.* and *Delay, Don't Deny*, but she has also become someone I am proud to call a friend. I 'met' Gin several years ago in an intermittent fasting Facebook group that I found after reading *Delay, Don't Deny*. But weirdly – and anyone who knows me knows that I do not believe in coincidences – what connected us was not that book but the fact that I later read that she had *self-published that book* (and it ultimately skyrocketed). That realization planted a seed that ultimately grew into the book you're now holding in your hands. Gin made me realize that all the crazy notes I had been keeping about all the things I was doing to get out of debt actually had the potential to become a book. After messaging back and forth with her about *that*, I decided that it would be.

Fast forward to a very entertaining podcast interview with her that included a crazy conversation about kilts (episode 298 of Gin's *Intermit-*

tent Fasting Stories), which led to a fantastic dinner with her on a trip to South Carolina for my son's power lifting competition. *That* dinner, in turn, led to an incredibly motivating "keep going" after she was kind enough to review my initial chapter outline and beginnings of this book, and today, to a friendship that I'm grateful for. Gin, I hope you know how very much you influenced everything about this book and made me realize that I could, so I did. Thank you.

And to Dylan, Nathan, Ashley, Angela, James, Raz, and Aaron, who were all kind enough to read my initial drafts, provide feedback, and/or listen to me talk endlessly about this book for the last two years: I sincerely adore you, and I thank you.

Finally, and most importantly, a tremendous and heartfelt thank you to Rich for allowing me to share so much of the story that we started together.

About the Author

S hanna Baritot lives in Upstate New York with her family, and holds degrees in Education and Business. She teaches as a college adjunct in addition to having a career that allows her to travel and meet some pretty incredible people.

When not spending time with her family and friends, she's usually hiking with her dog, playing bagpipes, or continually seeking out the perfect little coffee shop with a good friend or a great book. *The Debt Diet* is her first book.

www.ingramcontent.com/pod-product-compliance
Lightning Source LLC
Chambersburg PA
CBHW022107210326
41520CB00045B/438